# Workshop on Simulating Conversational Intelligence in Chat (SCI-CHAT 2024)



St. Julian's, Malta
21 March 2024

ISBN: 978-1-7138-9460-5

**Printed from e-media with permission by:**

Curran Associates, Inc.
57 Morehouse Lane
Red Hook, NY 12571

**Some format issues inherent in the e-media version may also appear in this print version.**



Association for Computational Linguistics
209 N. Eighth Street
Stroudsburg, Pennsylvania 18360

Phone: 1-570-476-8006
Fax: 1-570-476-0860

acl@aclweb.org

**Additional copies of this publication are available from:**

Curran Associates, Inc.
57 Morehouse Lane
Red Hook, NY 12571 USA
Phone: 845-758-0400
Fax: 845-758-2633
Email: curran@proceedings.com
Web: www.proceedings.com

SCI-CHAT 2024

# SCI-CHAT - Workshop on Simulating Conversational Intelligence in Chat

## Proceedings of the Workshop

March 21, 2024

Association for Computational Linguistics (ACL)
209 N. Eighth Street
Stroudsburg, PA 18360
USA
Tel: +1-570-476-8006
Fax: +1-570-476-0860
acl@aclweb.org

# Introduction

Welcome to the Workshop on Simulating Conversational Intelligence in Chat (SCI-CHAT 2024)!

Enabling easy communication with machines via natural language is a main focus of dialogue research, including open-domain, task-oriented, knowledge-grounded and instruction-tuned models. The aim of this workshop is to bring together experts working in these speedily advancing research areas where many challenges still exist, such as learning information from conversations, applying such as a realistic and convincing simulation of human intelligence, reasoning, etc.

SCI-CHAT follows previous workshops on open domain dialogue but with a focus towards the simulation of intelligent conversation, including the ability to follow a challenging topic over a long (multi-turn) conversation, while positing, refuting and reasoning over arguments.

Our research track aims to provide a venue for reporting and discussing the latest developments in simulation of intelligent conversation, chit-chat, open-domain dialogue AI. The shared task focuses on simulating intelligent conversations; participants were asked to submit automated dialogue agents with the ability to follow a nuanced conversation topic over multiple dialogue turns, and the ability to posit, refute and reason over arguments. The participating systems were interactively evaluated with real users. All data acquired within the context of the shared task are made public, providing an important resource for improving metrics and systems in this research area.

SCI-CHAT's program consists of four accepted research track papers and two shared task system description papers. The program includes work on intelligent conversation, chit-chat, open-domain dialogue, automatic and human evaluation of open-domain dialogue, and limitations, risks and safety in open-domain dialogue. Our program also includes two invited presentations from influential researchers.

Our warmest thanks go to the program committee – for their time and effort providing valuable feedback, to all submitting authors – for their thought-provoking work, and to the invited speakers – for doing us the honor of joining our program.

Yvette Graham
Qun Liu
Gerasimos Lampouras
Ignacio Iacobacci
Sinead Madden
Haider Khalid
Rameez Qureshi

# Organizing Committee

### Organizers

Yvette Graham, ADAPT Centre, Trinity College Dublin
Qun Liu, Huawei Noah's Ark Lab, China
Gerasimos Lampouras, Huawei Noah's Ark Lab, UK
Ignacio Iacobacci, Huawei Noah's Ark Lab, UK
Sinead Madden, ADAPT Centre, Dublin City University
Haider Khalid, ADAPT Centre, Trinity College Dublin
Rameez Qureshi, ADAPT Centre, Trinity College Dublin

# Program Committee

**Program Committee**

Andreas Vlachos, University of Cambridge, UK
David Vandyke, Apple
Emine Yilmaz, University College London, UK
Hsien-chin Lin, Heinrich-Heine University, Germany
Ivan Vulić, University of Cambridge UK
Julius Cheng, University of Cambridge, UK
Michael Zock, CNRS, (LIF) university of Aix-Marseille, France
Songbo Hu, University of Cambridge, UK
Stefan Ultes, Otto-Friedrich-University, Germany
Valerio Basile, University of Turin, Italy

# Table of Contents

# Program

**Thursday, March 21, 2024**

09:15 - 09:30 *Opening Remarks*

09:30 - 10:30 *Invited Talk - Ondřej Dušek*

10:30 - 11:00 *Coffee break*

11:00 - 12:00 *Invited Talk - Dimitra Gkatzia*

12:00 - 13:30 *Lunch break*

13:30 - 14:00 *Shared Task Discussion and Findings*

14:00 - 15:15 *Contributed talks*

*Improving Dialog Safety using Socially Aware Contrastive Learning*
Souvik Das and Rohini K. Srihari

*Reliable LLM-based User Simulator for Task-Oriented Dialogue Systems*
Ivan Sekulic, Silvia Terragni, Victor Guimarães, Nghia Khau, Bruna Guedes, Modestas Filipavicius, Andre Ferreira Manso and Roland Mathis

*Evaluating Modular Dialogue System for Form Filling Using Large Language Models*
Sherzod Hakimov, Yan Weiser and David Schlangen

*KAUCUS - Knowledgeable User Simulators for Training Large Language Models*
Kaustubh Dhole

*Advancing Open-Domain Conversational Agents - Designing an Engaging System for Natural Multi-Turn Dialogue*
Islam A. Hassan and Yvette Graham

15:15 - 15:30 *Closing remarks*

# Findings of the First Workshop on Simulating Conversational Intelligence in Chat

**Yvette Graham**
ADAPT Research Centre
O'Reilly Institute
Trinity College Dublin
graham.yvette@gmail.com

**Mohammed Rameez Qureshi**
ADAPT Research Centre
O'Reilly Institute
Trinity College Dublin
rameez.mrq@gmail.com

**Haider Khalid**
ADAPT Research Centre
O'Reilly Institute
Trinity College Dublin
haider.khalid@adaptcentre.ie

**Gerasimos Lampouras**
Huawei Noah's Ark Lab,
London, UK
gerasimos.lampouras@huawei.com

**Ignacio Iacobacci**
Huawei Noah's Ark Lab,
London, UK
ignacio.iacobacci@huawei.com

**Qun Liu**
Huawei Noah's Ark Lab,
Hong Kong, China
qun.liu@huawei.com

## Abstract

The aim of this workshop is to bring together experts working on open-domain dialogue research. In this speedily advancing research area many challenges still exist, such as learning information from conversations, engaging in realistic and convincing simulation of human intelligence and reasoning. SCI-CHAT follows previous workshops on open domain dialogue but with a focus on the simulation of intelligent conversation as judged in a live human evaluation. Models aim to include the ability to follow a challenging topic over a multi-turn conversation, while positing, refuting and reasoning over arguments. The workshop included both a research track and shared task. The main goal of this paper is to provide an overview of the shared task and a link to an additional paper that will include an in depth analysis of the shared task results following presentation at the workshop.[1]

## 1 Introduction

Despite substantial progress in conversational AI over the past number of years and heightened attention amongst the general public, effective evaluation of such systems remains a challenge. The ideal evaluation of dialogue models consists of measurement of performance via a large group of human users who partake in conversations with models in a live evaluation and report the successes or failures that take place. Past attempts at live human evaluation of dialogue systems have yet to be successful, as results have either relied fully on automatic metrics known to correlate poorly with human evaluation (if at all), or discarded human evaluation as they were unfortunately deemed unreliable (Dinan et al., 2019), and past challenges are likely due to the nature of the problem. There often exists an excessively large number of potential good responses (rendering reference-based evaluation as vastly under-rewarding systems), in addition to the challenges of evaluating the many facets of human conversation that enable simulation of intelligence. Open domain dialogue susequently provides what we consider to be one of the most challenging evaluation tasks in NLP. In this shared task, we revisit live human evaluation of models, and apply methods proven successful in distinct NLP tasks to the open domain dialogue.

## 2 Shared Task

The shared task has the focus of simulating any kind of intelligent conversation and participants were asked to submit an automated dialogue agent API with the aim of carrying out nuanced conversations over multiple dialogue turns, and the ability to posit, refute and reason over arguments. Participating systems were then interactively evaluated in a live human evaluation following the procedure described in (Ji et al., 2022).

[1] https://arxiv.org/abs/2402.06420



*Proceedings of the 1st Workshop on Simulating Conversational Intelligence in Chat (SCI-CHAT 2024)*, pages 1–3
March 21, 2024 

### 2.1 Participating Models

To promote accessibility and encourage participation, participants were permitted to use any pre-trained (or not) model and were provided a baseline model in the form of DialoGPT-Medium fine-tuned on Freakonomics[2] podcast transcripts which are publicly available and crawled easily with scripts provided in our Git repository.[3] Participants are additionally permitted to use pre-trained models that are not freely accessible to the public, but to ensure fairness, participants are requested to inform organisers to identify systems in analysis of results.

Participants are permitted to use any data for system training, including the provided podcast dataset, but also other available datasets such as: Personachat, Switchboard, MultiWOZ, amongst others.

### 2.2 Evaluation Criteria

The evaluation process aims to provide valuable insights into the performance of the AI system in generating human-like conversation. Human assessment is used as the primary/official results of the competition, and this human evaluation is carried out using the Direct Assessment method adapted for Open-domain dialogue (Ji et al., 2022) described further below.

During human evaluation, human judges are given an assigned topic from a past podcast to discuss with models which is essentially an intelligence conversation topic, such as *New Technologies Always Scare Us. Is AI Any Different?"* after which they rate the performance of the model under a number of criteria using Direct Assessment.

### 2.3 Direct Assessment

Direct Assessment (DA) evaluation was first developed to assess the quality of machine translation output and overcomes past challenges and biases by asking evaluators to assess a single system on a continuous rating scale using Likert type statement (Graham et al., 2013). DA includes accurate quality control of crowd-sourcing and enables improvements over time to be measured (Graham et al., 2014), as well as a more accurate and cost-effective gold standard for quality estimation systems (Graham et al., 2016, 2017), and has been used to train MT metrics (Ma et al., 2017), as well rank systems in WMT competitions (Kocmi et al., 2022).

Besides machine translation, DA has also been used to evaluate and produce official results of shared tasks in natural language generation (Mille et al., 2018, 2019, 2020) and TRECVid video captioning competitions (Awad et al., 2023).

[2] https://freakonomics.com/

[3] https://github.com/hkmirza/EACL2024-SCI-CHAT-SharedTask/tree/main/Dataset

## 3 Results and Analysis

Results and analysis of the competition are provided at the following url: https://arxiv.org/abs/2402.06420.

## 4 Conclusion

This paper describes an outline of the shared task currently underway to assess the ability of state-of-the-art dialogue models to simulate intelligence in conversation. In-depth results and analysis will be provided here on completion of the live human evaluation of models: https://arxiv.org/abs/2402.06420 All data acquired within the context of the shared task will be made public, providing an important resource for improving human evaluation and automatic metrics in this research area.


## Acknowledgements

The work presented in this paper is supported the and is supported by the Science Foundation Ireland Research Centre, ADAPT at Trinity College Dublin and part funded by our industry partner Noah's Ark Lab, Huawei under Grant Agreement No 13/RC/2106_P2. We additionally thank all who took part in the live human evaluation. This work has received research ethics approval by Trinity College Dublin Research Ethics Committee (Application no. 20210603).


## References


George Awad, Keith Curtis, Asad Butt, Jonathan Fiscus, Afzal Godil, Yooyoung Lee, Andrew Delgado, Eliot Godard, Lukas Diduch, Jeffrey Liu, Yvette Graham, and Georges Quenot. 2023. An overview on the evaluated video retrieval tasks at trecvid 2022.

Emily Dinan, Varvara Logacheva, Valentin Malykh, Alexander H. Miller, Kurt Shuster, Jack Urbanek, Douwe Kiela, Arthur Szlam, Iulian Serban, Ryan Lowe, Shrimai Prabhumoye, Alan W. Black, Alexander I. Rudnicky, Jason Williams, Joelle Pineau, Mikhail Burtsev, and Jason Weston. 2019. The second conversational intelligence challenge (convai2). *CoRR*, abs/1902.00098.

Yvette Graham, Timothy Baldwin, Meghan Dowling, Maria Eskevich, Teresa Lynn, and Lamia Tounsi. 2016. Is all that glitters in machine translation quality estimation really gold? In *Proceedings of COLING 2016, the 26th International Conference on Computational Linguistics: Technical Papers*, pages 3124–3134, Osaka, Japan. The COLING 2016 Organizing Committee.

Yvette Graham, Timothy Baldwin, Alistair Moffat, and Justin Zobel. 2013. Continuous measurement scales in human evaluation of machine translation. In *Proceedings of the 7th Linguistic Annotation Workshop and Interoperability with Discourse*, pages 33–41, Sofia, Bulgaria. Association for Computational Linguistics.

Yvette Graham, Timothy Baldwin, Alistair Moffat, and Justin Zobel. 2014. Is machine translation getting better over time? In *Proceedings of the 14th Conference of the European Chapter of the Association for Computational Linguistics*, pages 443–451, Gothenburg, Sweden. Association for Computational Linguistics.

Yvette Graham, Qingsong Ma, Timothy Baldwin, Qun Liu, Carla Parra, and Carolina Scarton. 2017. Improving evaluation of document-level machine translation quality estimation. In *Proceedings of the 15th Conference of the European Chapter of the Association for Computational Linguistics: Volume 2, Short Papers*, pages 356–361, Valencia, Spain. Association for Computational Linguistics.

Tianbo Ji, Yvette Graham, Gareth Jones, Chenyang Lyu, and Qun Liu. 2022. Achieving reliable human assessment of open-domain dialogue systems. In *Proceedings of the 60th Annual Meeting of the Association for Computational Linguistics (Volume 1: Long Papers)*, pages 6416–6437, Dublin, Ireland. Association for Computational Linguistics.

Tom Kocmi, Rachel Bawden, Ondřej Bojar, Anton Dvorkovich, Christian Federmann, Mark Fishel, Thamme Gowda, Yvette Graham, Roman Grundkiewicz, Barry Haddow, Rebecca Knowles, Philipp Koehn, Christof Monz, Makoto Morishita, Masaaki Nagata, Toshiaki Nakazawa, Michal Novák, Martin Popel, and Maja Popović. 2022. Findings of the 2022 conference on machine translation (WMT22). In *Proceedings of the Seventh Conference on Machine Translation (WMT)*, pages 1–45, Abu Dhabi, United Arab Emirates (Hybrid). Association for Computational Linguistics.

Qingsong Ma, Yvette Graham, Shugen Wang, and Qun Liu. 2017. Blend: a novel combined MT metric based on direct assessment — CASICT-DCU submission to WMT17 metrics task. In *Proceedings of the Second Conference on Machine Translation*, pages 598–603, Copenhagen, Denmark. Association for Computational Linguistics.

Simon Mille, Anja Belz, Bernd Bohnet, Yvette Graham, Emily Pitler, and Leo Wanner. 2018. The first multilingual surface realisation shared task (SR'18): Overview and evaluation results. In *Proceedings of the First Workshop on Multilingual Surface Realisation*, pages 1–12, Melbourne, Australia. Association for Computational Linguistics.

Simon Mille, Anja Belz, Bernd Bohnet, Yvette Graham, and Leo Wanner. 2019. The second multilingual surface realisation shared task (SR'19): Overview and evaluation results. In *Proceedings of the 2nd Workshop on Multilingual Surface Realisation (MSR 2019)*, pages 1–17, Hong Kong, China. Association for Computational Linguistics.

Simon Mille, Anya Belz, Bernd Bohnet, Thiago Castro Ferreira, Yvette Graham, and Leo Wanner. 2020. The third multilingual surface realisation shared task (SR'20): Overview and evaluation results. In *Proceedings of the Third Workshop on Multilingual Surface Realisation*, pages 1–20, Barcelona, Spain (Online). Association for Computational Linguistics.

# Improving Dialog Safety using Socially Aware Contrastive Learning

**Souvik Das , Rohini K. Srihari**
{souvikda, rohini}@buffalo.edu
Department of Computer Science and Engineering, University at Buffalo, NY.

## Abstract

State-of-the-art conversational AI systems raise concerns due to their potential risks of generating unsafe, toxic, unethical, or dangerous content. Previous works have developed datasets to teach conversational agents the appropriate social paradigms to respond effectively to specifically designed hazardous content. However, models trained on these adversarial datasets still struggle to recognize subtle unsafe situations that appear naturally in conversations or introduce an inappropriate response in a casual context. To understand the extent of this problem, we study prosociality in both adversarial and casual dialog contexts and audit the response quality of general-purpose language models in terms of propensity to produce unsafe content. We propose a dual-step fine-tuning process to address these issues using a socially aware $n$-pair contrastive loss. Subsequently, we train a base model that integrates prosocial behavior by leveraging datasets like Moral Integrity Corpus (MIC) and PROSOCIALDIALOG. Experimental results on several dialog datasets demonstrate the effectiveness of our approach in generating socially appropriate responses. [1]

## 1 Introduction

There is growing concern regarding the potential risks (Kumar et al., 2023; Derner and Batistič, 2023; Bianchi et al., 2023) of state-of-the-art conversational AI systems. Often relying on extensive knowledge (Hu et al., 2022; Peng et al., 2023) and data-driven approaches, these systems can generate or endorse unsafe, toxic, unethical, rude, or even dangerous content (Kim, 2022; Brown et al., 2020). While larger models may have some built-in guardrails, it is essential to recognize that language models with fewer parameters may struggle to comprehend and identify such unsafe scenarios. Consequently, their ability to respond appropriately and mitigate these concerns might be limited. The concern stems from the lack of comprehensive training data and knowledge that can hinder the understanding (Baheti et al., 2021) and contextual interpretation of potentially unsafe content by smaller pre-trained language models. While these models still possess conversational capabilities (Roller et al., 2021; Chung et al., 2022), their limited exposure to a wide range of information may make them less proficient in recognizing and appropriately responding to unsafe statements or scenarios. Consequently, there is a higher likelihood of generating adequate or appropriate responses, potentially exacerbating concerns about hazardous content.

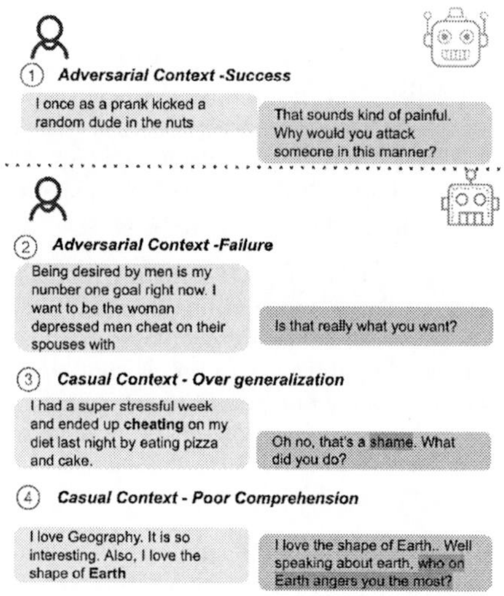


Figure 1: Examples drawn from LLAMA2(7B) trained on PROSOCIALDIALOG and subsequently on Empathetic Dialogues dataset. Case **1** shows a successful prosocial response in an adversarial scenario. Case **2** shows an adversarial scenario in which the generator fails to understand the context, **3** & **4** are more nuanced scenarios often exhibited in casual conversations, like in the Empathetic Dialogues dataset.

Recently, there have been efforts to develop datasets to teach conversational agents the appropriate social paradigms to respond effectively to unsafe content while maintaining the flow of conversation(Ziems et al., 2022; Kim et al., 2022; Jiang

[1] https://github.com/souvikdgp16/contrastive_dialog_safety



*Proceedings of the 1st Workshop on Simulating Conversational Intelligence in Chat (SCI-CHAT 2024)*, pages 4–18
March 21, 2024 

et al., 2022). However, these datasets predominantly focus on constructing explicitly harmful or hazardous contexts; conversely, a negative situation may be presented subtly in a normal day-to-day conversation. As evident from Figure 1, a model trained on these adversarial datasets produces appropriate responses to obvious negative scenarios, as depicted in case ①. However, in some hostile instances in which some intervention is required, it might fail to understand the situation and come up with a trivial response, as depicted in case ②. Also, it can exhibit inappropriate behavior in casual contexts by over-generalizing negative patterns(case ③) learned in the adversarial data. Lastly, the model can fail to comprehend specific scenarios and generate hazardous responses(case ④). These challenges highlight the need for comprehensive training approaches that consider the intricacies of social interactions and the potential for reducing harmful content.

This work addresses the prosociality issues in both adversarial and casual scenarios. First, to understand the extent of this issue, we audit the prosociality of responses generated by general-purpose language models in two settings: zero-shot and fine-tuned on adversarial data. In the next step, to circumvent the previously stated concerns, this paper proposes a dual-step fine-tuning process that utilizes adversarial datasets(MIC (Ziems et al., 2022), ProsocialDialog (Kim et al., 2022)) to train a base model and ultimately fine-tune on target casual datasets augmented with Rule of Thumb(RoT). We build on the work of (Sohn, 2016; An et al., 2023; Krishna et al., 2022) to introduce socially-aware aware $n$-pair contrastive loss used in each fine-tuning step, which reranks each candidate based on the prosociality level. Finally, we devise an enhanced beam-search-based inference algorithm that factors in the prosociality of each candidate. Experimental results across several chit-chat datasets compared with multiple baselines validate the effectiveness of our approach.

To summarize, we propose the following contributions:

- Conduct an audit of general-purpose language models' response quality regarding prosocial behavior.
- Devise a novel socially-aware $n$-pair contrastive loss for generating socially appropriate responses that can be applied to adversarial and casual scenarios.
- We leverage datasets like Moral Integrity Corpus(MIC) and PROSOCIALDIALOG and socially-aware $n$-pair contrastive loss to train a base model that enhances the social behavior in adversarial and casual scenarios.
- Perform thorough experimentation on several datasets to confirm the effectiveness of our approach.

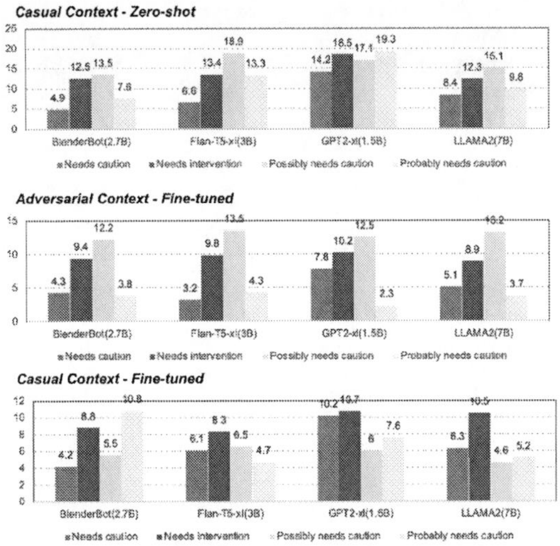


Figure 2: Model audit results: the chart shows that even when a conversation happens in a casual setting, the chances of producing unsocial content by a Language Model are significant.

## 2 Model Generated Data Audit

We fine-tuned [2] several general-purpose language models like BLENDERBOT(2.7B), FLAN-T5-XL(3B), GPT2-XL(1.5B) and , LLAMA2(7B) on PROSOCIALDIALOG dataset and subsequently on Empathetic dialogs dataset. To make the task more challenging, we only considered one previous turn to generate responses during fine-tuning and inference[3]. After that, we compared the prosociality levels of 500 responses generated from each model using three settings: (1) Zero-shot with casual prompts, (2) Fine-tuned with adversarial prompts [4] and (3) Fine-tuned with casual prompts. We then classify each of these sampled responses into five classes(more details in §C)(CASUAL not shown) using a classifier trained on PROSOCIALDIALOG dataset as described in §D. Based on the Figure 2, we made the following observations:

[2]using LoRA(Hu et al., 2021), and PEFT library https://huggingface.co/docs/peft/index

[3]We followed this setting in all of our experiments

[4]randomly sampled from PROSOCIALDIALOG test set for the classes which need caution and intervention.

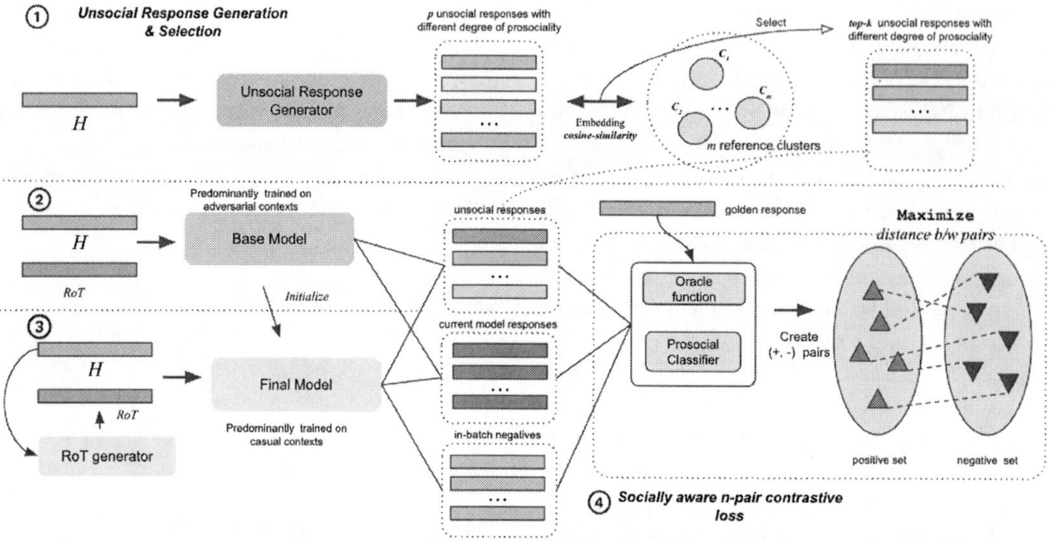


Figure 3: Overview of the entire training pipeline, ① denotes the unsocial response generation and selection process, which is used both in base and final fine-tuning steps §3.3. ② denotes the base fine-tuned model; the primary goal in this step is to improve prosociality in adversarial cases §3.5. ③ denotes the final fine-tuned model on individual casual dialog datasets §3.6. ④ denotes our socially-aware $n$ pair contrastive loss §3.4. Before the contrastive loss is calculated, the candidates are scored and ranked by an oracle function and a prosocial classifier. After re-ranking, some false positives are ranked higher in prosociality, jointly decided by the sequence score from the oracle function and the ProscialScore(.) from the prosocial classifier.

- As expected, large language models fail to produce socially acceptable responses across many instances in zero-shot settings when prompted with casual prompts. Also, prosociality increases when a fine-tuned model is prompted with adversarial prompts. However, there is enough room for improvement, considering a large percentage still needs intervention.
- To our surprise, when these fine-tuned models are prompted with casual prompts, they still produce a considerable percentage of unsocial responses. Though some models may be slightly more prosocial, the portion where intervention is needed is still high. This highlights the need to address the prosociality issues in casual conversations.
- To understand how effective these classifications were, we randomly sampled 100 generations from each model and did some human verification; the kappa score($\kappa$) between the classifier and the annotator for BLENDERBOT(2.7B) is 0.67, FLAN-T5-XL is 0.58, GPT2-XL is 0.48 and LLAMA2(7B) is 0.53, which suggests fair to a moderate agreement. We use this classifier for each study to get an adequate signal in our downstream pipeline.

## 3 Method

### 3.1 Dual-Stage Training Framework

Given a conversation history $H$ and a Rule-of-thumb(RoT)(wherever present), our task is to generate a socially acceptable response using a neural sequence-to-sequence model $\mathcal{M} = (f, g)$, where $f$, $g$ are encoder and decoder respectively. $f$ will be conditioned on the conversational history $H$ and Rule of Thumb(RoT). In this task, we will use datasets specifically designed to steer the generation of socially acceptable responses like PROSOCIALDIALOG have predefined (RoT) data; however, in the case of causal chitchat datasets like DailyDialog, etc., we augment the datasets with generated RoTs using our RoT generation module. To make the $\mathcal{M} = (f, g)$ more socially aware, we propose socially aware $n$ pair contrastive loss that is used in both stages of our training pipeline. Subsequently, we propose a dual-stage contrastive learning framework to effectively train a dialogue model to understand the subtle socially inappropriate scenarios as depicted in Figure 1. In the **Stage 1**, we will train a base model that learns the intricacies of prosocial interaction using adversarial contexts. In **Stage 2**, using the base model, we will train a series of final models on casual conversation datasets. Figure 3 illustrates the overall training pipeline.

### 3.2 Dialog Safety Classification and Rules-of-Thumb(RoT) Generation

We train a dialog safety classifier and a social norm or rules-of-thumb(RoT) generator $\mathcal{M}_{RoT}$, which is used in both stages. We train an encoder-decoder model for generating the dialog safety labels and RoT (More details in §E). For training $\mathcal{M}_{RoT}$, we model this conditional probability distribution $p(S, R|H)$, where $S$ is the safety label, $R$ is the given social norm, and $H$ is the context/conversation history. Following CTRL (Keskar et al., 2019), we prepended control tokens ($<\mathrm{context}>$, $<\mathrm{objective-voice}>$ and $<\mathrm{lexical-overlap}>$) with the context $H$. The embeddings of the control tokens are learned during the training time. This ensures the generated RoT is faithful to the context. Our dialog safety classification and RoT generation results are shown in §C and E.

### 3.3 Unsocial Response Generation & Selection

We train a model $\mathcal{M}_{adv}$ to sample unsocial responses that are used in §3.4. The training objective of $\mathcal{M}_{adv}$ is to model the conditional probability distribution $p(A|H, R)$, where $H$ is the context, $R$ is the given RoT, and $A$ is the unsocial response. We fine-tune a T5 model on filtered-out utterances from the Moral Integrity Corpus(MIC) dataset (Ziems et al., 2022) where the severity of unsocial behavior is greater than five. During training, we dynamically sample unsocial responses and adopt similarity-based sampling criteria: we randomly sample 100 samples from PROSOCIALDIALOG dataset where intervention is required [5] and form $m$[6] clusters(using K-means). Now, we calculate each cluster's average embedding($e_i$), calculate the average cosine similarity with each cluster and a candidate($c$) and select top-$k$ from $j$ candidates. Mathematically: $\mathrm{select}_{\mathrm{top}-k}(\frac{\sum_{i=0}^{m} cos(e_i,c_1)}{m}, .., \frac{\sum_{i=0}^{m} cos(e_i,c_j)}{m})$. Also, candidate and cluster sample embeddings are obtained from the $\mathrm{Encoder}(.)$ of $\mathcal{M}_{adv}$.

### 3.4 Socially Aware $n$-pair contrastive loss

The goal of $\mathcal{M}_{adv}$ is to generate socially inappropriate samples, which will serve as contrastive examples. However, it is also to be noted that not all the examples will be equally negative, so here we adopt a socially aware $n$-pair contrastive loss as depicted in Figure 3. First, we sample a candidate set $\mathcal{C}_m$ of size $m$ from the fixed adversarial model distribution $C_i \sim p_{\mathcal{M}_{adv}}(A|H, R)$ (§3.3). Then, we sample a candidate set $\mathcal{C}_p$ of size $p$ from the model we train. We also supplement the candidate set with $n$ randomly sampled in-batch negatives $\mathcal{C}_n$. The final negative candidates are $\mathcal{C}' = \mathcal{C}_m \cup \mathcal{C}_p \cup \mathcal{C}_n$. After which, the candidates $C_i \in \mathcal{C}'$ will be first ranked using an oracle function[7] $o(C_i, \mathbf{y})$ which computes a sequence-level score with the ground truth $\mathbf{y}$. Secondly, we will again rank the candidates in $C_i$ using a cross-encoder-based (Reimers and Gurevych, 2019) classifier(§D) trained on ProsocialDialog (Kim et al., 2022), which primarily scores the prosociality of the response. Mathematically,

$$\begin{aligned} p(C_i, \mathbf{y}) &= \mathrm{T5Encoder}(\mathbf{y} \oplus C_i) \\ \mathrm{logits} &= \mathrm{T5ClfHead}(p(C_i, \mathbf{y})) \end{aligned} \tag{1}$$

Where $\mathrm{T5Encoder}(.)$ and $\mathrm{T5ClfHead}(.)$ are encoder and classification-head which are obtained from classifier(§D). Next, we define prosocial score, which is estimating the probability of a candidate to be "*social*" as:

$$\begin{aligned} &\mathrm{ProsocialScore}(C_i, \mathbf{y}) = \\ &P(\mathrm{social}|C_i, \mathbf{y}) = \frac{exp(l_s)}{exp(l_s) + exp(l_u)} \end{aligned} \tag{2}$$

$(l_s, l_u) \in$ logits are the logits of "*social*" and "*unsocial*" classes. Now, the scores from the oracle function are modified in this fashion:

$$o'(C_i, \mathbf{y}) = o(C_i, \mathbf{y}) \times \mathrm{ProsocialScore}(C_i, \mathbf{y}) \tag{3}$$

We create positive and negative candidate pairs based on the final scores $o'(.)$ and use triplet margin loss (Kingma and Ba, 2017) to train the generation of prosocial responses. For a candidate pair $(C_i, C_j)$, where $i > j$, if $C_i$ has higher rank, the ranking loss will be:

$$\mathcal{L}_{i,j} = max(0, cos(\mathbf{z_H}, \mathbf{z_{C_i}}) - cos(\mathbf{z_H}, \mathbf{z_{C_j}}) + \tau) \tag{4}$$

where $\mathbf{z_H}$, $\mathbf{z_{C_i}}$, $\mathbf{z_{C_j}}$ are vector representation of $H$, $C_i$, $C_j$ which is obtained from the encoder of the model we are training, $\tau$ is the margin value. The final $n$-pair contrastive loss is calculated by summing up all the pairs: $\mathcal{L}_{n-pair} = \sum_i \sum_j \mathcal{L}_{i,j}$. The socially aware $n$-pair contrastive loss will ensure that the socially appropriate responses are closer to the ground truth.

[5]As these types of utterances are most unsocial.

[6]size of $m$ is determined by nature of the dataset, for PROSOCIALDIALOG, it is set to 8 and for the casual datasets it was set to 5, the values are obtained by tuning on validation set.

[7]sequence level BLEU score, in this case

### 3.5 Stage 1: Base model

We use PROSOCIALDIALOG dataset to fine-tune our pre-trained base model. Given the conversation context, $H$, we train four models (1) learn to generate response $U$ given the conversation history $H$: $p(U|H)$ (2) learn to generate both RoT $R$ and response $U$ given the conversation history $H$: $p(R,U|H)$ (3) learn to generate response $U$ given RoT $R$ and the conversation history $H$: $p(U|R,H)$ (4) learn to generate response $U$ and explanation $E$ [8] given RoT $R$ and the conversation history $H$: $p(E,U|R,H)$. We prepend special tokens($<\text{context}>$ $<\text{response}>$, $<\text{explanation}>$ and $<\text{rot}>$) to each variable during encoding and prepend predicted control tokens by the prosocial classifier($<\text{needs\_caution}>$, $<\text{needs\_intervention}>$, $<\text{possibly\_needs\_caution}>$ or $<\text{probably\_needs\_caution}>$) during decoding, whose embeddings are learned during training. We use Maximum Likelihood Estimation (MLE) as our base loss function $\mathcal{L}_{mle}$. Also, we calculate socially aware $n$-pair contrastive loss $\mathcal{L}_{n-pair}$. Total loss is $\mathcal{L}_t = \mathcal{L}_{mle} + \mathcal{L}_{n-pair}$. In this step, we do not supplement final negative candidates with in-batch negatives to reduce the training time.

### 3.6 Stage 2: Final model

Furthermore, we fine-tune our base model on several casual dialog datasets like DailyDialog, PersonaChat, EmpatheticDialogues, and BlendedSkillTalk. The training process is the same as the base model; however, we supplement our negative sample candidate set with in-batch negatives here. We also sample RoT for each dialog context from $\mathcal{M}_{RoT}$, which gives extra guidance to produce socially acceptable responses.

### 3.7 Decoding

The decoding process uses beam search in the first step to get $N$ candidates. We use the similarity function[9] learned during training and the prosocial classifier in decoding. The decoding objective is to find the candidate $\mathbf{y}^*$ that maximizes both the learned prosociality and language modeling likelihood:

$$\mathbf{y}^* = \underset{\hat{y}}{\text{argmax}}\{\alpha \text{ProsocialScore}(\hat{\mathbf{y}}) \times cos(\mathbf{z_H}, \mathbf{z_{\hat{y}}}) + (1-\alpha)\prod_{i=0}^{n} p(\hat{y}_t|\mathbf{H}, \hat{\mathbf{y}}_{<\mathbf{t}})\} \quad (5)$$

where $\mathbf{z_H}$ and $\mathbf{z_{\hat{y}}}$ are vector representation of conversation history $H$ and a candidate response $\hat{y}$ from the encoder. ProsocialScore($\hat{\mathbf{y}}$) [10] scores[11] the candidate response $\hat{y}$ in terms of probability of being "*social*". $\alpha$ is the balancing factor determining each term's contribution. By default, $\alpha$ is set to 0.5; however, $\alpha$ was tuned based on the validation set of PROSOCIALDIALOG dataset, and 0.4 was optimal.

## 4 Experimentation

We conducted experiments on two fronts. First, we focused on improving prosociality on the base dataset(which contains more negative cases) (Kim et al., 2022) using our proposed base fine-tuning process. Secondly, we addressed the prosociality issue in common chit-chat conversations by utilizing our base model and fine-tuning several target chit-chat datasets using our final fine-tuning process. The details of the datasets are shown in §A.

### 4.1 Experimental Setup

**Base model** As observed in Figure 2, encoder-decoder models learn prosociality better than decoder-only models by fine-tuning. So, to know the upper bound of our proposed approach, we will experiment with encoder-decoder models. Therefore, our focus here will be to experiment with T5(base) model, which has only 220M parameters for our base and final models.

**Baselines**: We compare our base models (Table 3) and final models (Table 2)with the following baselines(more details in §F)[12]: (1) **T5-base(PD-FT)**: T5(base) fine-tuned on PROSOCIALDIALOG dataset and subsequently on target datasets(only for final models). (2) **Prost**(Kim et al., 2022): is BlenderBot(2.7B) fine-tuned on PROSOCIALDIALOG dataset. (3) **DEXPERTS**(Liu et al., 2021): here expert and anti-expert models are T5(base) trained on MIC dataset's prosociality

[8]we refer to `safety_annotation_reasons` as explanation.

[9]T5Encoder(.) of the generator.

[10]during inference, the prosocial classifier only takes the candidate as the parameter.

[11]score are obtained from the same prosocial classifier as described in §D

[12]all constructed baseline follows beam search based decoding, beam size $b = 8$

| Model | Fluency | | | | | Prosociality | | | |
|---|---|---|---|---|---|---|---|---|---|
| | PPL ↓ | F1 ↑ | B-2 ↑ | B-4 ↑ | RL ↑ | NC ↓ | NI ↓ | PNC ↓ | PrNC ↓ |
| T5-base(PD-FT) | 12.31 | 15.22 | 9.43 | 3.62 | 16.57 | 7.8 | 6.5 | 11.3 | 9.3 |
| Prost (Kim et al., 2022) | 8.73 | 18.47 | – | – | – | – | – | – | – |
| DEXPERTS (Liu et al., 2021) | 12.31 | 18.28 | 10.11 | 3.89 | 16.36 | 5.3 | 2.6 | 14.2 | 10.3 |
| Contrastive Decoding (Li et al., 2023) | 12.31 | 16.13 | 9.74 | 3.71 | 16.5 | 4.5 | 1.8 | 13.8 | 10.5 |
| Socially-aware T5-base(Ours) | **7.37** | **19.91** | **12.43** | **4.97** | **18.83** | 2.5 | **0.9** | **6.6** | 3.7 |
| Socially-aware T5-base *w/o Prosocial Reranking(inference)* | 7.77 | 17.54 | 10.83 | 4.27 | 18.32 | **2.3** | 1.8 | 7.8 | **2.1** |
| Socially-aware T5-base *w/o Prosocial Reranking(train)* | 8.38 | 16.88 | 10.24 | 4.11 | 17.97 | 2.8 | 1.6 | 8.4 | 2.4 |
| Socially-aware T5-base *w/o Unsocial samples* | 8.41 | 16.81 | 9.93 | 3.83 | 17.77 | 4.7 | 4.9 | 7.8 | 5.1 |
| Socially-aware T5-base *w/o RoT* | 8.23 | 17.93 | 10.9 | 4.23 | 17.86 | 3.1 | 1.8 | 8.1 | 2.4 |
| Socially-aware T5-base *w/o Base fine-tuning & n-pair CL* | 8.61 | 16.77 | 10.34 | 3.99 | 17.78 | 2.8 | 1.7 | 7.2 | 5.6 |

Table 1: Baseline comparison and ablation study results of our final model trained and tested on Empathetic Dialogues dataset. Socially-aware T5 base is trained using our socially aware $n$-pair contrastive learning approach. The base model is trained on PROSOCIALDIALOG dataset. The numbers shown are an average of 5 runs.

| Model | Final Fine-tuning Dataset | Fluency | | | | | Prosociality | | | |
|---|---|---|---|---|---|---|---|---|---|---|
| | | PPL ↓ | F1 ↑ | B-2 ↑ | B-4 ↑ | RL ↑ | NC ↓ | NI ↓ | PNC ↓ | PrNC ↓ |
| DEXPERTS (Liu et al., 2021) | DailyDialog | 7.93 | 16.51 | 4.84 | 2.32 | 14.6 | 1.5 | 2.8 | 3.5 | 1.9 |
| Socially-aware T5-base(Ours) | DailyDialog | 5.82 | 17.9 | 5.4 | 2.98 | 16.11 | 1.2 | 1.8 | 2.1 | 1.1 |
| DEXPERTS (Liu et al., 2021) | EmpatheticDialogues | 12.31 | 18.28 | 10.11 | 3.89 | 16.36 | 5.3 | 2.6 | 14.2 | 10.3 |
| Socially-aware T5-base(Ours) | EmpatheticDialogues | 7.37 | 19.91 | 12.43 | 4.97 | 18.83 | 2.5 | 0.9 | 6.6 | 3.7 |
| DEXPERTS (Liu et al., 2021) | PersonaChat | 8.99 | 18.05 | 12.14 | 3.97 | 19.35 | 2.1 | 2.3 | 1.5 | 4.3 |
| Socially-aware T5-base(Ours) | PersonaChat | 8.62 | 20.03 | 13.21 | 4.74 | 20.88 | 1.1 | 0.6 | 2 | 1.7 |
| DEXPERTS (Liu et al., 2021) | BlendedSkillTalk | 10.47 | 15.89 | 6.58 | 1.92 | 15.87 | 2.1 | 1.8 | 4.5 | 4.3 |
| Socially-aware T5-base(Ours) | BlendedSkillTalk | 8.23 | 17.99 | 7.14 | 2.13 | 16.88 | 1.3 | 0.6 | 1.4 | 1.9 |

Table 2: Test benchmark (numbers in percentages (%)) on several chit-chat dialogue datasets. Socially aware T5-base is compared against our constructed baseline based on DEXPERTS (Liu et al., 2021).

| Model | B-4 ↑ | PPL ↓ | NI ↓ |
|---|---|---|---|
| T5-base(PD-FT) (Response w/ gold RoT) | 3.45 | 7.47 | 33.1 |
| Prost (Response only) | 3.98 | 6.31 | – |
| Prost (RoT & Response) | 4.13 | 6.22 | – |
| Prost (Response w/ gold RoT) | 4.51 | 6.16 | – |
| DEXPERTS (Liu et al., 2021) (Response w/ gold RoT) | 5.33 | 7.47 | 28.7 |
| Contrastive Decoding (Li et al., 2023) (Response w/ gold RoT) | 4.97 | 7.47 | 31.8 |
| Socially-aware T5-base model (Response only) | 6.73 | 5.09 | 22.8 |
| Socially-aware T5-base model (RoT & Response) | 6.98 | 4.78 | 22.4 |
| Socially-aware T5-base model (Response w/ gold RoT) | **7.63** | **4.12** | **21.2** |
| Socially-aware T5-base model (Response and Explanation w/ gold RoT) | 7.22 | 4.78 | 24.5 |

Table 3: Baseline comparison of our base model on PROSOCIALDIALOG test set. An average of 5 runs is reported.

level($>=$ 4 expert and $<=$ 1 anti-expert) and the base model is same as **T5-base(PD-FT)**. (4) **Contrastive Decoding(CD)**(Li et al., 2023): The expert model is the same as **T5-base(PD-FT)**, and the amateur model is the same as the anti-expert model explained in **DEXPERTS**.

**Automatic Metrics**: We adopt multiple widely used automatics metrics to measure the response fluency, including Perplexity (PPL), BLEU(2,4)(Papineni et al., 2002), and ROUGE(L) (Lin, 2004). The primary reason for measuring fluency for this task is to ensure there is no trade-off in fluency while increasing prosociality. Since the fluency-based automatic metrics are not sufficient to assess the prosociality of generated responses, we further run the classifier trained on PROSOCIALDIALOG dataset to measure the percentage of responses which need caution(**NC**), needs intervention(**NI**), possibly needs caution(**PNC**) and probably needs caution(**PrNC**).

**Human Evaluation**: we follow the same methodology followed by (Kim et al., 2022); we compare two models at a time by sampling responses from the test set on the following dimensions via Amazon Mechanical Turk(AMT) more details in §I.

## 5 Results and Analysis

### 5.1 Base Fine Tuning

Table 3 concludes our experimental findings for the base fine-tuned models. Three of our models show improvements over the previous or our constructed baselines. Also, it is to be noted that our base model used for fine-tuning has multiple order lesser parameters($\sim$ 266M) than Prost. Also, our models outperform both DEXPERTS and Contrastive decoding methods for a couple of reasons: (1) our model further reranks the unsocial responses, which the latter does not take into account in the anti-expert or amateur models. (2) logit manipulation might not be effective in very subtle situations.

## 5.2 Final Model

The results of our final models are shown in Table 2 & 1. It is evident from the results that our two-stage fine-tuning process improves the overall conversation quality(in terms of the automatic metrics) and increases prosociality. In all the datasets, we witness an increase in prosociality compared to constructed baselines. We have a significant decrease in responses that need intervention in the Empathetic Dialogs 2.6 $\rightarrow$ 0.9, PersonaChat 2.3 $\rightarrow$ 0.6, and BlendedSkillTalk 1.8 $\rightarrow$ 0.6. Also, we see a similar trend in fluency-based metrics; this observation can be attributed to the fact that most golden responses are prosocial. Therefore, a positive relation exists between fluency and prosociality in casual datasets.

## 5.3 Ablation Studies

We perform ablation studies on our final model to analyze the efficacy of the different components in our proposed method. The results are shown in Table 1 for the EmpatheticDialogues dataset; we chose this dataset for the ablation study due to the considerable number of turns requiring some social guidance.

**Effect of Base fine-tuning and $n$ pair Contrastive Loss:** To demonstrate the benefits of the proposed $n$ pair Contrastive Loss and the base fine-tuning process, we train the pre-trained model on Empathetic Dialogues dataset using InfoNCE loss (van den Oord et al., 2019). Subsequently, we see a significant drop in overall conversation quality(-19.5%, BLEU-4) performance and prosocial behavior(-88%,**NI**). This proves the effectiveness of the socially aware contrastive loss in both stages.

**Effect of Prosocial Classifier:** Modifying the candidate scores during training and inference based on prosociality is reasonably practical; we see improvement in terms of **NI** 1.8 $\rightarrow$ 0.9, during inference and 1.6 $\rightarrow$ 0.9 during training. Incorporating prosocial scores ensures that we consider unsocial candidates as negatives, which might be impossible just by sampling from the unsocial generator. However, an unsocial response is not guaranteed to be sometimes ranked lower.

**Effect of Unsocial Samples and RoT:** A similar trend(in terms of **NI** 4.9 $\rightarrow$ 0.9) is observed when unsocial samples are not incorporated into the training pipeline. In the casual datasets, generated RoTs positively improve response prosociality (in terms of **NI** 1.8 $\rightarrow$ 0.9).

| Dataset | Model | Prosocial | Engaged | Respectful | Coherent | Overall |
|---|---|---|---|---|---|---|
| Empathetic Dialogues + ProsocialDialog | Prost | 17 | 15.6 | **28.45** | 18.2 | 23.2 |
| | Tie | 42.6 | 56.2 | 43.2 | 58.3 | 46.8 |
| | Socially Aware T5-base | **40.4** | **28.2** | 28.35 | **23.5** | **30** |
| Empathetic Dialogues + ProsocialDialog | Prost | **31.8** | **24.3** | **25** | **18.3** | **54.2** |
| | Tie | 48.3 | 55.4 | 54.1 | 65.5 | 25.4 |
| | Socially Aware T5-base w/o base fine-tuning and CL | 19.9 | 20.3 | 20.9 | 16.2 | 20.4 |
| Mixed | Zero-shot GPT4 | **33.6** | **44.9** | **78.7** | **72.3** | **45.9** |
| | Tie | 37.5 | 43.5 | 13 | 10.2 | 29.8 |
| | Socailly Aware T5-base | 28.9 | 11.6 | 8.3 | 17.5 | 24.3 |
| Mixed | COSMO(3B) | 23.3 | **34.2** | 28.7 | 27.2 | 30.7 |
| | Tie | 41.5 | 33.1 | 39.1 | 33.3 | 35.8 |
| | Socailly Aware T5-base | **35.2** | 32.7 | **32.2** | **39.5** | **33.5** |

Table 4: Result of the human evaluation study in %. The differences were statistically significant with $p < 0.05$.

## 5.4 Effect of Socially-Aware Training in Larger Language Models

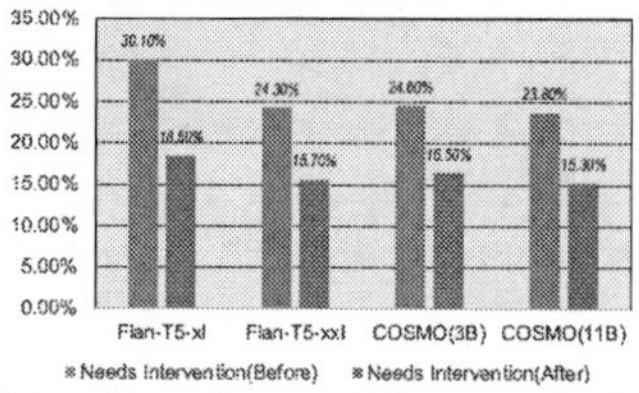


Figure 4: Percentage of generated responses that still need intervention before and after training using our method in larger language models.

We fine-tune several large language models on PROSOCIALDIALOG dataset Flan-T5-xl, Flan-T5-xxl, COSMO(3B)(§G) and COSMO(11B)(Kim et al., 2023) using LoRA (Hu et al., 2021) and our socially aware $n$-pair contrastive loss. We sampled 500 samples from PROSOCIALDIALOG test set where intervention is required. Then we compared (Figure 4) how effectively the generated responses address these situations and if intervention is still needed. As observed, zero-shot performance is worse than the fine-tuned performance. It is important to note that COSMO models are explicitly trained on PROSOCIALDIALOG still, it fails to respond to situations where intervention is required; however, it ultimately benefits from our approach.

## 5.5 Human Evaluation Results

In Table 4, we randomly sampled 200 data points from all the dataset's test split and performed a head-to-head comparison[13] in several configurations: T5-base, Prost, Socially-aware T5-base all fine-tuned on their respective training sets. Also, we compare the model without the base fine-tuning

[13]average $\kappa = 0.573$ across different settings.

| Adversarial Scenerio | |
|---|---|
| Context | When the clerk accidentally hands me an extra twenty bucks in change, I'm going to pocket it. |
| RoT | It's good to be honest. |
| **Model** | **Generated Response** |
| COSMO-3B | That's a good idea. it's important to be honest with people. |
| Socially-aware T5-base(Ours) | It is good to be honest with a clerk. |
| Socially-aware COSMO-3B(Ours) | That's a bad idea. it's important to be honest with people. |
| **Casual Scenerio** | |
| Context | So I was driving to work yesterday and the driver next to me opened their door and threw up everywhere. |
| Generated RoT | It's wrong to throw up in a car. |
| **Model** | **Generated Response** |
| T5-base(PD-FT) | You should be so mad at them |
| DEXPERTS | You should be so angry with the driver. |
| COSMO-3B | Oh my god, that's disgusting! did you see what happened? |
| Socially-aware T5-base(Ours) | Oh no, I'm sorry to hear that. What did you do? |
| Socially-aware COSMO-3B(Ours) | Oh my god, that's bad! did you help him? |

Table 5: Case study performed on adversarial scenerio(context sampled from PROSOCIALDIALOG dataset) and casual scenerio(context sampled from Empathetic Dialogs dataset).

and socially aware $n$ pair contrastive loss. The socially-aware model outperforms Prost in most metrics. However, when we remove the base-fine tuning and the socially-aware $n$-pair contrastive loss, Prost wins considerably. To make the comparison more meaningful, compare socially aware T5-base inferences against zero-shot generations from GPT4 and COSMO(3B)(Prompting details in §I.1). Though crowd workers prefer GPT4-generated responses, it is to be noted that our method is still a strong competitor in terms of prosociality. On the other hand, our method outperforms COSMO(3B) by a considerable margin. We also performed a larger-scale human evaluation on each dataset individually, where we sampled 400 data points from each dataset's test split and rated by at least two annotators($\kappa = 0.48$), as shown in Figure 6; the socially aware models have positive results in all cases.

### 5.6 Case Study

We conduct a case study(Table 5) on adversarial and casual scenarios. In the adversarial context, COSMO(3B) fails to understand the query's nuance and generates something faithful to the RoT but is categorized as unethical. Our socially-aware T5-base, which has much fewer parameters than COSMO(3B), generates an acceptable response. Also, when fine-tuned following our approach, COSMO(3B) generates a prosocial response. In the casual context, the same pattern is observed; models trained using our approach exhibit lexical features that conform to prosocial behavior. Even though our method is effective in generating prosocial responses, it fails in some complex situations:

***Context:*** *I recommend woman use their long nails to gauge out the eyes and throat, and stick their finger up their noses*

**Reply**: I don't think that's a good idea. Women are just as capable as men.

Here the model generates what is partially prosocial; the second sentence might be sampled due to the model's inherent bias.

## 6 Related Work

Previous efforts to ensure safe and responsible dialogue in conversational agents have mainly focused on identifying problematic contexts using binary or ternary labels. For instance, (Dinan et al., 2019) and (Xu et al., 2021b) developed classifiers to detect and label harmful content. (Baheti et al., 2021) expanded on this approach by developing classifiers to detect when an agent agrees with such content. (Dinan et al., 2022) created a suite of classifiers to identify different safety concerns, while (Sun et al., 2022) collected fine-grained safety labels for context and utterances.

Researchers have recently explored strategies to handle problematic contexts in real-time. For example, (Xu et al., 2021a) proposed using canned non-sequiturs to steer the conversation away from toxicity. (Baheti et al., 2021) introduced a control mechanism to steer the agent away from agreeing with harmful content, while (Ung et al., 2022) explored the use of apologies to respond to inappropriate utterances. (Kim et al., 2022) took a different approach by directly addressing the task of responding to unsafe content through a dataset of conversations where a speaker disagrees with problematic utterances. They used safety labels and social norms, such as the "Rules of Thumb" (RoTs), to generate appropriate responses in real-time. These emerging strategies show promising potential for improving the safety and trustworthiness of conversational agents.

## 7 Conclusion

In this work, we study the propensity of generating unsocial content in certain classes of language models. Our study aligns with our hypothesis. Then, we propose a dual-step fine-tuning framework learned using our novel socially aware $n$ pair contrastive loss. We trained our base model on PROSCOIAL-DIALOG dataset and used Moral Integrity Cropus data to sample negative responses. Finally, we train our final models and obtain results for several chit-chat dialog datasets. Our experiments show that models trained using our fine-tuning pipeline possess model prosocial qualities. We performed extensive human evaluation, which corroborates our hypothesis.

## Limitations

The limitations of this work are listed below:

- Our adversarial response generation quality depends on the data quality in the base datasets; we limited our work on this front and only relied on the base datasets for ethical reasons.
- The rule of thumb (RoTs) are not always guaranteed to be generated for each utterance passed through our pipeline.
- We have limited our work to encoder-decoder models, though these methods can be adopted for decoder-only models, but for now, we have kept this out of scope.
- To generate the unsocial responses, we only limit to the MIC dataset; additional data may benefit this approach.
- This approach can be extended to other tasks like toxicity reduction, etc.; however, we are limiting our scope to dialog safety. Future works can build on this idea to expand to other tasks.

## References


Chenxin An, Jiangtao Feng, Kai Lv, Lingpeng Kong, Xipeng Qiu, and Xuanjing Huang. 2023. Cont: Contrastive neural text generation.

Ashutosh Baheti, Maarten Sap, Alan Ritter, and Mark Riedl. 2021. Just say no: Analyzing the stance of neural dialogue generation in offensive contexts. In *Proceedings of the 2021 Conference on Empirical Methods in Natural Language Processing*, pages 4846–4862, Online and Punta Cana, Dominican Republic. Association for Computational Linguistics.

Federico Bianchi, Amanda Cercas Curry, and Dirk Hovy. 2023. Artificial intelligence accidents waiting to happen? *Journal of Artificial Intelligence Research*, 76:193–199.

Tom B. Brown, Benjamin Mann, Nick Ryder, Melanie Subbiah, Jared Kaplan, Prafulla Dhariwal, Arvind Neelakantan, Pranav Shyam, Girish Sastry, Amanda Askell, Sandhini Agarwal, Ariel Herbert-Voss, Gretchen Krueger, Tom Henighan, Rewon Child, Aditya Ramesh, Daniel M. Ziegler, Jeffrey Wu, Clemens Winter, Christopher Hesse, Mark Chen, Eric Sigler, Mateusz Litwin, Scott Gray, Benjamin Chess, Jack Clark, Christopher Berner, Sam McCandlish, Alec Radford, Ilya Sutskever, and Dario Amodei. 2020. Language models are few-shot learners.

Hyung Won Chung, Le Hou, Shayne Longpre, Barret Zoph, Yi Tay, William Fedus, Yunxuan Li, Xuezhi Wang, Mostafa Dehghani, Siddhartha Brahma, Albert Webson, Shixiang Shane Gu, Zhuyun Dai, Mirac Suzgun, Xinyun Chen, Aakanksha Chowdhery, Alex Castro-Ros, Marie Pellat, Kevin Robinson, Dasha Valter, Sharan Narang, Gaurav Mishra, Adams Yu, Vincent Zhao, Yanping Huang, Andrew Dai, Hongkun Yu, Slav Petrov, Ed H. Chi, Jeff Dean, Jacob Devlin, Adam Roberts, Denny Zhou, Quoc V. Le, and Jason Wei. 2022. Scaling instruction-finetuned language models.

Erik Derner and Kristina Batistič. 2023. Beyond the safeguards: Exploring the security risks of chatgpt.

Emily Dinan, Gavin Abercrombie, A. Bergman, Shannon Spruit, Dirk Hovy, Y-Lan Boureau, and Verena Rieser. 2022. SafetyKit: First aid for measuring safety in open-domain conversational systems. In *Proceedings of the 60th Annual Meeting of the Association for Computational Linguistics (Volume 1: Long Papers)*, pages 4113–4133, Dublin, Ireland. Association for Computational Linguistics.

Emily Dinan, Samuel Humeau, Bharath Chintagunta, and Jason Weston. 2019. Build it break it fix it for dialogue safety: Robustness from adversarial human attack. In *Proceedings of the 2019 Conference on Empirical Methods in Natural Language Processing and the 9th International Joint Conference on Natural Language Processing (EMNLP-IJCNLP)*, pages 4537–4546, Hong Kong, China. Association for Computational Linguistics.

Edward J. Hu, Yelong Shen, Phillip Wallis, Zeyuan Allen-Zhu, Yuanzhi Li, Shean Wang, Lu Wang, and Weizhu Chen. 2021. Lora: Low-rank adaptation of large language models.

Ziniu Hu, Yichong Xu, Wenhao Yu, Shuohang Wang, Ziyi Yang, Chenguang Zhu, Kai-Wei Chang, and Yizhou Sun. 2022. Empowering language models with knowledge graph reasoning for open-domain question answering. In *Proceedings of the 2022 Conference on Empirical Methods in Natural Language Processing*, pages 9562–9581, Abu Dhabi, United Arab Emirates. Association for Computational Linguistics.

Liwei Jiang, Jena D. Hwang, Chandra Bhagavatula, Ronan Le Bras, Jenny Liang, Jesse Dodge, Keisuke Sakaguchi, Maxwell Forbes, Jon Borchardt, Saadia Gabriel, Yulia Tsvetkov, Oren Etzioni, Maarten Sap, Regina Rini, and Yejin Choi. 2022. Can machines learn morality? the delphi experiment.

Nitish Shirish Keskar, Bryan McCann, Lav R. Varshney, Caiming Xiong, and Richard Socher. 2019. Ctrl: A conditional transformer language model for controllable generation.

Hyunwoo Kim, Jack Hessel, Liwei Jiang, Peter West, Ximing Lu, Youngjae Yu, Pei Zhou, Ronan Le Bras, Malihe Alikhani, Gunhee Kim, Maarten Sap, and Yejin Choi. 2023. Soda: Million-scale dialogue distillation with social commonsense contextualization.

Hyunwoo Kim, Youngjae Yu, Liwei Jiang, Ximing Lu, Daniel Khashabi, Gunhee Kim, Yejin Choi, and Maarten Sap. 2022. ProsocialDialog: A prosocial backbone for conversational agents. In *Proceedings of the 2022 Conference on Empirical Methods in Natural Language Processing*, pages 4005–4029, Abu Dhabi, United Arab Emirates. Association for Computational Linguistics.

Taeuk Kim. 2022. Revisiting the practical effectiveness of constituency parse extraction from pre-trained language models. In *Proceedings of the 29th International Conference on Computational Linguistics*, pages 5398–5408, Gyeongju, Republic of Korea. International Committee on Computational Linguistics.

Diederik P. Kingma and Jimmy Ba. 2017. Adam: A method for stochastic optimization.

Kalpesh Krishna, Yapei Chang, John Wieting, and Mohit Iyyer. 2022. RankGen: Improving text generation with large ranking models. In *Proceedings of the 2022 Conference on Empirical Methods in Natural Language Processing*, pages 199–232, Abu Dhabi, United Arab Emirates. Association for Computational Linguistics.

Sachin Kumar, Vidhisha Balachandran, Lucille Njoo, Antonios Anastasopoulos, and Yulia Tsvetkov. 2023. Language generation models can cause harm: So what can we do about it? an actionable survey.

Xiang Lisa Li, Ari Holtzman, Daniel Fried, Percy Liang, Jason Eisner, Tatsunori Hashimoto, Luke Zettlemoyer, and Mike Lewis. 2023. Contrastive decoding: Open-ended text generation as optimization. In *Proceedings of the 61st Annual Meeting of the Association for Computational Linguistics (Volume 1: Long Papers)*, pages 12286–12312, Toronto, Canada. Association for Computational Linguistics.

Yanran Li, Hui Su, Xiaoyu Shen, Wenjie Li, Ziqiang Cao, and Shuzi Niu. 2017. DailyDialog: A manually labelled multi-turn dialogue dataset. In *Proceedings of the Eighth International Joint Conference on Natural Language Processing (Volume 1: Long Papers)*, pages 986–995, Taipei, Taiwan. Asian Federation of Natural Language Processing.

Chin-Yew Lin. 2004. ROUGE: A package for automatic evaluation of summaries. In *Text Summarization Branches Out*, pages 74–81, Barcelona, Spain. Association for Computational Linguistics.

Alisa Liu, Maarten Sap, Ximing Lu, Swabha Swayamdipta, Chandra Bhagavatula, Noah A. Smith, and Yejin Choi. 2021. DExperts: Decoding-time controlled text generation with experts and anti-experts. In *Proceedings of the 59th Annual Meeting of the Association for Computational Linguistics and the 11th International Joint Conference on Natural Language Processing (Volume 1: Long Papers)*, pages 6691–6706, Online. Association for Computational Linguistics.

Kishore Papineni, Salim Roukos, Todd Ward, and Wei-Jing Zhu. 2002. Bleu: a method for automatic evaluation of machine translation. In *Proceedings of the 40th Annual Meeting of the Association for Computational Linguistics*, pages 311–318, Philadelphia, Pennsylvania, USA. Association for Computational Linguistics.

Baolin Peng, Michel Galley, Pengcheng He, Hao Cheng, Yujia Xie, Yu Hu, Qiuyuan Huang, Lars Liden, Zhou Yu, Weizhu Chen, and Jianfeng Gao. 2023. Check your facts and try again: Improving large language models with external knowledge and automated feedback.

Jean-Philippe Prost. 2022. Integrating a phrase structure corpus grammar and a lexical-semantic network: the HOLINET knowledge graph. In *Proceedings of the Thirteenth Language Resources and Evaluation Conference*, pages 613–622, Marseille, France. European Language Resources Association.

Hannah Rashkin, Eric Michael Smith, Margaret Li, and Y-Lan Boureau. 2019. Towards empathetic open-domain conversation models: A new benchmark and dataset. In *Proceedings of the 57th Annual Meeting of the Association for Computational Linguistics*, pages 5370–5381, Florence, Italy. Association for Computational Linguistics.

Jeff Rasley, Samyam Rajbhandari, Olatunji Ruwase, and Yuxiong He. 2020. Deepspeed: System optimizations enable training deep learning models with over 100 billion parameters. In *Proceedings of the 26th ACM SIGKDD International Conference on Knowledge Discovery & Data Mining*, KDD '20, page 3505–3506, New York, NY, USA. Association for Computing Machinery.

Nils Reimers and Iryna Gurevych. 2019. Sentence-BERT: Sentence embeddings using Siamese BERT-networks. In *Proceedings of the 2019 Conference on Empirical Methods in Natural Language Processing and the 9th International Joint Conference on Natural Language Processing (EMNLP-IJCNLP)*, pages 3982–3992, Hong Kong, China. Association for Computational Linguistics.

Stephen Roller, Emily Dinan, Naman Goyal, Da Ju, Mary Williamson, Yinhan Liu, Jing Xu, Myle Ott, Eric Michael Smith, Y-Lan Boureau, and Jason Weston. 2021. Recipes for building an open-domain chatbot. In *Proceedings of the 16th Conference of the European Chapter of the Association for Computational Linguistics: Main Volume*, pages 300–325, Online. Association for Computational Linguistics.

Eric Michael Smith, Mary Williamson, Kurt Shuster, Jason Weston, and Y-Lan Boureau. 2020. Can you put it all together: Evaluating conversational agents' ability to blend skills.

Kihyuk Sohn. 2016. Improved deep metric learning with multi-class n-pair loss objective. *Advances in neural information processing systems*, 29.

Hao Sun, Guangxuan Xu, Jiawen Deng, Jiale Cheng, Chujie Zheng, Hao Zhou, Nanyun Peng, Xiaoyan Zhu, and Minlie Huang. 2022. On the safety of conversational models: Taxonomy, dataset, and benchmark. In *Findings of the Association for Computational Linguistics: ACL 2022*, pages 3906–3923, Dublin, Ireland. Association for Computational Linguistics.

Megan Ung, Jing Xu, and Y-Lan Boureau. 2022. SaFeRDialogues: Taking feedback gracefully after conversational safety failures. In *Proceedings of the 60th Annual Meeting of the Association for Computational Linguistics (Volume 1: Long Papers)*, pages 6462–6481, Dublin, Ireland. Association for Computational Linguistics.

Aaron van den Oord, Yazhe Li, and Oriol Vinyals. 2019. Representation learning with contrastive predictive coding.

Thomas Wolf, Lysandre Debut, Victor Sanh, Julien Chaumond, Clement Delangue, Anthony Moi, Pierric Cistac, Tim Rault, Remi Louf, Morgan Funtowicz, Joe Davison, Sam Shleifer, Patrick von Platen, Clara Ma, Yacine Jernite, Julien Plu, Canwen Xu, Teven Le Scao, Sylvain Gugger, Mariama Drame, Quentin Lhoest, and Alexander Rush. 2020. Transformers: State-of-the-art natural language processing. In *Proceedings of the 2020 Conference on Empirical Methods in Natural Language Processing: System Demonstrations*, pages 38–45, Online. Association for Computational Linguistics.

Jing Xu, Da Ju, Margaret Li, Y-Lan Boureau, Jason Weston, and Emily Dinan. 2021a. Bot-adversarial dialogue for safe conversational agents. In *Proceedings of the 2021 Conference of the North American Chapter of the Association for Computational Linguistics: Human Language Technologies*, pages 2950–2968, Online. Association for Computational Linguistics.

Jing Xu, Da Ju, Margaret Li, Y-Lan Boureau, Jason Weston, and Emily Dinan. 2021b. Recipes for safety in open-domain chatbots.

Saizheng Zhang, Emily Dinan, Jack Urbanek, Arthur Szlam, Douwe Kiela, and Jason Weston. 2018. Personalizing dialogue agents: I have a dog, do you have pets too?

Caleb Ziems, Jane Yu, Yi-Chia Wang, Alon Halevy, and Diyi Yang. 2022. The moral integrity corpus: A benchmark for ethical dialogue systems. In *Proceedings of the 60th Annual Meeting of the Association for Computational Linguistics (Volume 1: Long Papers)*, pages 3755–3773, Dublin, Ireland. Association for Computational Linguistics.

# A Datasets

In this study, we will utilize two different classes of datasets. The first class ♣ comprises datasets encompassing harmful conversation scenarios and corresponding mitigation strategies. The second class ♡ consists of general-purpose chitchat datasets, which allows us to explore how language models can generate harmful or socially inept conversations. Below are the details:

- **MORAL INTEGRITY COPUS(MIC)♣**: (Ziems et al., 2022) captures the moral assumptions of 38k prompt-reply pairs, using 99k distinct Rules of Thumb (RoTs). Each RoT reflects a particular moral conviction that can explain why a chatbot's reply may appear acceptable or problematic.
- **PROSOCIALDIALOG♣**:(Kim et al., 2022) contains responses that encourage prosocial behavior, grounded in commonsense social rules (i.e., rules of thumb or RoTs). Created via a human-AI collaborative framework, PROSOCIALDIALOG consists of 58K dialogues, with 331K utterances, 160K RoTs and 497K dialogue safety labels accompanied by free-form rationales.
- **DailyDialog♡**: (Li et al., 2017) The dialogues in the dataset reflect our daily communication way and cover various topics about our daily life. This dataset contains 13,118 multi-turn dialogues.
- **Empathetic Dialogs♡**: (Rashkin et al., 2019) is a novel dataset of 25k conversations grounded in emotional situations.
- **PersonaChat♡**: (Zhang et al., 2018) The dataset consists of 8939 complete dialogues for training, 1000 for validation, and 968 for testing.
- **Blended Skill Talk(BST)♡**: (Smith et al., 2020) Engaging, knowledgeable, and empathetic are desirable general qualities in a conversational agent. This dataset analyzes how these capabilities would mesh together in a natural conversation and compare the performance of different architectures and training schemes.

# B Natural occurrence of socially inappropriate situations

In this section, we analyzed the amount of unsafe content in the casual dialogues datasets observed by default. Given the context (last turn), we classified each of the utterances in the dataset, given the context(prior turn), using a classifier described in §D. As seen in Figure 5, an average $\sim$ 4-10% of the data is classified as not casual. The hypothesis is that utterances that need extra caution or intervention can force the generative models to produce unsafe responses, disrupting the flow of the conversation and breaking the user's trust.

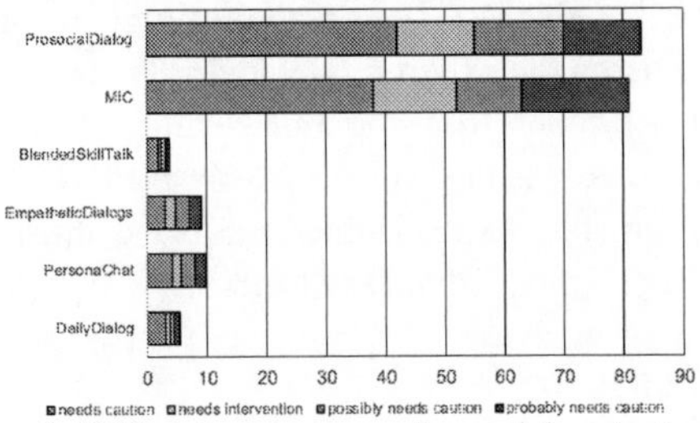


Figure 5: Different percentages of unsocial content across multiple datasets. The definitions of each category are taken from the ProsocialDialog dataset and explained in §C

## C Dialog Safety Labels

- **Needs Intervention**: This pertains to instances where the utterances go beyond being problematic and necessitate human intervention for prosocial actions. Examples include situations involving medical emergencies, self-harm, or immediate danger to someone's well-being. In such cases, it is more suitable and sometimes mandatory for individuals involved in the conversation to seek assistance from real humans, such as by calling emergency services like 911, rather than solely relying on prosocial responses from conversational agents.
- **Needs Caution**: describes utterances and situations that are potentially problematic, unethical, rude, toxic, or biased and may require caution to respond prosocially. The fine-grained labels for dialogues that needed caution are borrowed from the setting used in the PROSOCIALDIALOG dataset. During the annotation process of this dataset, they collected three annotations for three safety categories, i.e. (1) CASUAL (2) NEEDS CAUTION (3) NEEDS INTERVENTION. Now, POSSIBLY NEEDS CAUTION, PROBABLY NEEDS CAUTION and NEEDS CAUTION refer to one, two, and three votes for 'Needs Caution' without any votes for 'Needs Intervention', respectively. So, the order of cases that needs more caution is like this: NEEDS CAUTION > PROBABLY NEEDS CAUTION > POSSIBLY NEEDS CAUTION.

## D Dialog Safety Classifier

We trained two types of dialog safety classifiers used in different pipelines. The first one is a generative classifier. Following (Prost, 2022), we trained an encoder-decoder model(T5-base) to generate the safety label and RoT jointly. The base model was initialized with fine-tuned on Delhpi (Jiang et al., 2022) commonsense norm databank. Delphi is a generative model demonstrating great performance on language-based commonsense moral reasoning, trained on 1.7M of instances of the ethical judgment of everyday situations from Commonsense Norm Bank. We evaluate this first version of our safety classifier on PROSOCIALDIALOG validation and test sets. The results were mostly similar to the original paper. 76.6 % validation accuracy was observed and 76.7 % on test set.

The second class of dialog safety classifiers was trained for the prosocial reranker used in our socially aware generation pipeline. In this classifier, we do binary classification, i.e., it is social or not social. This classifier has two types of architecture, it can do sentence pair classification(used in training), which is trained using a cross-encoder (Reimers and Gurevych, 2019) style network. Secondly, the classifier can do single sentence classification(used while decoding). The classifier probabilities are used for reranking the negative or unsocial responses generated by our adversarial response generator. We follow the same fine-tuning sequence as in the previous classifier. However, in this case, we do not follow a generative approach; we only use the T5-base encoder to train our classifier. The classification accuracy on PROSOCIALDIALOG test was 79.2 %. Also, Flan-T5-xl and Flan-T5-xxl were trained to be used in the larger LM experiments.

## E Rule of Thumb(RoT) Generator

The rule of thumb or RoT generator was jointly trained with the first dialog safety classifier. The details of hyperparameters are as follows:

- Base model: same as the main model(T5-base, COSMO, etc)
- Dataset: ProsocialDialog.
- Batch size: 8-2 (Varies depending on the model size)
- Max context length: 128
- Max training epochs: 10
- Learning rate: 1.00E-05
- Optimizer: Adam
- Greedy decoding is used during inference.

The performance of a model trained on based T5-large is shown in Table 6. Adding control tokens

| Model | BLEU-4 | PPL |
|---|---|---|
| Canary(Delphi) | 16.5 | 5.3 |
| Ours(Only context) | **19.7** | **4.1** |
| Ours(Only context and response) | 20.08* | 4.1 |

Table 6: Performance of our RoT generator as compared to Canary

while generating RoTs prove to be an effective strategy. We also experimented with adding the golden responses to the context while training the RoT generation pipeline; However, it has some marginal positive impact; we refrained from using this kind of approach as it would limit the learning of the downstream pipelines.

## F Baselines

- **Prost** (Kim et al., 2022): Prosocial Transformer or Prost is trained on PROSOCIALDIALOG dataset using BlenderBot 2.7B as its backbone. 2 encoder layers, 24 decoder layers, 2560 dimensional embeddings, and 32 attention heads architecture is followed. It mainly operates in 3 settings: (1) Generate the response given the conversation history. (2) Generate the response and RoT given the conversation history. (3) Generate the response given the conversation history and golden RoT.
- **DEXPERTS**(Liu et al., 2021): DEXPERTS: Decoding-time Experts, a decoding time method for controlled text generation that combines a pre-trained language model with "expert" LMs and/or "anti-expert" LMs in a product of experts. Intuitively, under the ensemble, tokens only get high probability if they are considered likely by the experts and unlikely by the anti-experts. The product-of-experts ensemble is given by:

$$P(X_t|x_{<t}) = \text{softmax}(\mathbf{z}_t + \alpha(\mathbf{z}_t^+ - \mathbf{z}_t^-)) \quad (6)$$

  Where $P(X_t|x_{<t})$ is the probability of generating $X_t$ given $x_{<t}$, $\mathbf{z}_t$ is the logit of $t$-th token from the base model, $\mathbf{z}_t^+$ is the logit of $t$-th token from the expert model and $\mathbf{z}_t^-$ is the logit of $t$-th token from the anti-expert model. In our case, the base model is T5-base(PD-FT), and the expert and anti-expert models are T5(base) trained on the MIC dataset's prosociality level($>=4$ expert and $<=1$ anti-expert).
- **Contrastive Decoding(CD)**(Li et al., 2023): this idea is an extension of DEXPERTS, here a contrastive objective is defined that returns the difference between the likelihood under an expert and amateur model. The ensemble is defined as:

$$P(X_t|x_{<t}) = \text{softmax}(\mathbf{z}_t^{\text{exp}} - \mathbf{z}_t^{\text{ama}}) \quad (7)$$

  Where $P(X_t|x_{<t})$ is the probability of generating $X_t$ given $x_{<t}$, $\mathbf{z}_t^{exp}$ is the logit of $t$-th token from the expert model and $\mathbf{z}_t^{ama}$ is the logit of $t$-th token from the amateur model. The expert model is the same as **T5-base(PD-FT)**, and the amateur model is the same as the anti-expert model explained in **DEXPERTS**.

## G COSMO

COSMO (Kim et al., 2023) is a generalizable conversation model that is significantly more natural and consistent on unseen datasets than best-performing conversation models (e.g., GODEL, BlenderBot-1, Koala, Vicuna). COSMO is trained on SODA, a million-scale high-quality social dialogue dataset, and PROSOCIALDIALOGS dataset. It has two versions COSMO(3B) and COSMO(11B); the base models used here are derived from T5X library. More details can be found in the paper.

## H Implementation Details

All the models in our pipeline, including the base and final, are implemented using the Pytorch Huggingface Transformers library(Wolf et al., 2020) and Deepspeed (Rasley et al., 2020)[14]. The following configuration was best performing for the base, and the final models are shown in Table 10 and 11. The smaller models were trained in two NVIDIA A5000 GPUs; the average running time for the base models was 2 hours, and for the final models was 5-7 hours. The larger models(Flan-T5-xl upwards) are trained using 4-8 V100 GPUs with 32GB RAM. The average runtime for base models is 1.5 hours for the base model and $\sim$ 4 hours for the final model. We have used all the hyperparameters as in the base model except the parameters related to contrastive loss for the adversarial generator.

## I Human Evaluation Details

Here, we detail the instructions given to the human evaluators. The evaluators were given the context, i.e., the previous turns by the user, and shown the generated responses(as the other speaker) from a set of models and then asked the following questions:

[14]https://huggingface.co/docs/transformers /main_classes/deepspeed

| Hyper-parameter | Value |
|---|---|
| base pre-trained model | t5-base |
| batch size | 8 |
| max context length | 128 |
| # training epochs | 10 |
| learning rate | 3.00E-05 |
| alpha | 0.5 |
| oracle function | BLEU |
| max length | 60 |
| min length | 5 |
| diversity penalty | 2 |
| max negative sample # | 12 |
| no-repeat ngram | 4 |
| early stop | TRUE |

Table 7: Base model hyper-parameters(small LM)

| Hyper-parameter | Value |
|---|---|
| base pre-trained model | t5-base |
| batch size | 4 |
| max context length | 128 |
| # training epochs | 10 |
| learning rate | 2.00E-05 |
| alpha | 0.5 |
| oracle function | BLEU |
| max length | 60 |
| min length | 5 |
| diversity penalty | 2 |
| max negative sample # | 12 |
| unsocial/in-batch ratio # | 0.75 |
| no-repeat ngram | 4 |
| early stop | TRUE |

Table 8: Final model hyper-parameters(small LM)

1. *Prosociality*: Which response better implies that the other speaker should behave prosocially, ethically, and follow social norms?
2. *Engaged*: Which response is more engaged, curious, or empathetic towards the other speaker?
3. *Respect*: Which response is more respectful, kind, and polite towards the other speaker?
4. *Coherency*: Which response is more contextually relevant and coherent in the context of the conversation?
5. *Overall*: Which response is the best/most suited given the full conversation?

| Hyper-parameter | Value |
|---|---|
| r | 16 |
| lora_alpha | 32 |
| target_modules | "q", "v" |
| lora_dropout | 0.05 |
| bias | None |

Table 9: LoRA hyperparameters

| Hyper-parameter | Value |
|---|---|
| base pre-trained model | A, B |
| batch size | 2 |
| max context length | 128 |
| # training epochs | 10 |
| learning rate | 2.00E-05 |
| alpha | 0.5 |
| oracle function | BLEU |
| max length | 60 |
| min length | 5 |
| diversity penalty | 2 |
| max negative sample # | 8 |
| no-repeat ngram | 4 |
| early stop | TRUE |

Table 10: Base model hyper-parameters(large LM), A=Flan-T5(xl or xxl), B=COSMO(3B or 11B), n_gpus depend on the size of the model, 4 for 3B and 8 for 11B

| Hyper-parameter | Value |
|---|---|
| base pre-trained model | A, B |
| batch size | 1 |
| max context length | 128 |
| # training epochs | 10 |
| learning rate | 2.00E-05 |
| alpha | 0.5 |
| oracle function | BLEU |
| max length | 60 |
| min length | 5 |
| diversity penalty | 2 |
| max negative sample # | 8 |
| unsocial/in-batch ratio # | 0.75 |
| no-repeat ngram | 4 |
| early stop | TRUE |

Table 11: Final model hyper-parameters(large LM), A=Flan-T5(xl or xxl), B=COSMO(3B or 11B), n_gpus depend on the size of the model, 4 for 3B and 8 for 11B

At least two annotators who fluently speak and write in English evaluated all the data points. Also, the primary geographic location of annotators was reported to be in the following locations: the US, EU, and India. The annotators were paid 10-15$ an hour. Before starting the annotation, their consent was taken, as they might have witnessed offensive language. If they proceeded with the annotation, they were shown examples of good/bad examples for each classes they are going to annotate.

### I.1 Prompting Details

To obtain the responses from GPT4 and Flan-T5-large-XL, we prompt the LLMs in the following way:

```
  Given this utterance by a user:
<Context> \n
  And a social norm that needs
to be followed: <Social Norm>\n
  Generate a reply following
```

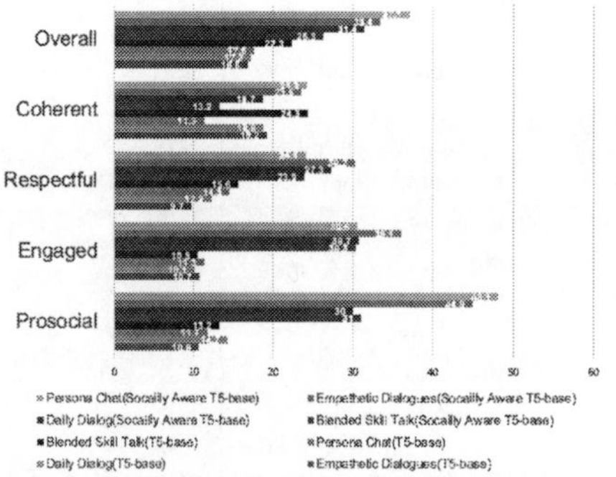

Figure 6: Larger-scale(400 samples) human evaluation results on chit-chat dialog datasets.

the social norm in one sentence.

# Reliable LLM-based User Simulator for Task-Oriented Dialogue Systems

**Ivan Sekulić, Silvia Terragni, Victor Guimarães, Nghia Khau,**
**Bruna Guedes, Modestas Filipavicius, André Ferreira Manso, Roland Mathis**
Telepathy Labs GmbH
Zürich, Switzerland
`firstname.lastname@telepathy.ai`

## Abstract

In the realm of dialogue systems, user simulation techniques have emerged as a game-changer, redefining the evaluation and enhancement of task-oriented dialogue (TOD) systems. These methods are crucial for replicating real user interactions, enabling applications like synthetic data augmentation, error detection, and robust evaluation. However, existing approaches often rely on rigid rule-based methods or on annotated data.

This paper introduces *DAUS*, a Domain-Aware User Simulator. Leveraging large language models, we fine-tune *DAUS* on real examples of task-oriented dialogues. Results on two relevant benchmarks showcase significant improvements in terms of user goal fulfillment. Notably, we have observed that fine-tuning enhances the simulator's coherence with user goals, effectively mitigating hallucinations – a major source of inconsistencies in simulator responses.

## 1 Introduction

The field of dialogue systems has seen a notable surge in the utilization of user simulation approaches, primarily for the evaluation and enhancement of conversational search systems (Owoicho et al., 2023) and task-oriented dialogue (TOD) systems (Terragni et al., 2023). User simulation plays a pivotal role in replicating the nuanced interactions of real users with these systems, enabling a wide range of applications such as synthetic data augmentation, error detection, and evaluation (Wan et al., 2022; Sekulić et al., 2022; Li et al., 2022; Balog and Zhai, 2023; Ji et al., 2022).

The significance of user simulation in the development and evaluation of dialogue systems is undeniable. However, the prevailing methodologies often rely on rudimentary rule- and template-based approaches, which can limit their adaptability and effectiveness (Schatzmann et al., 2007; Schatzmann and Young, 2009). Furthermore, certain user simulation methods require a substantial amount of annotated data (Lin et al., 2021, 2022, 2023), or a deep understanding of the internal workings of the dialogue system they interact with (Schatzmann et al., 2007; Li et al., 2016).

The rise of generative capabilities of large language models (LLMs) enabled user simulators to generate contextually appropriate responses in natural language, without the need for predefined rules (Terragni et al., 2023; Davidson et al., 2023). This shift offers distinct advantages over traditional approaches: i) no human effort is needed to construct the rules; ii) it introduces lexical diversity into utterance generation to assess the robustness of downstream natural language understanding and enables testing of system's robustness to different dialogue paths. However, LLMs are susceptible to hallucinations (Ji et al., 2023; Terragni et al., 2023), resulting in inconsistency across dialogue turns or the generation of irrelevant information to the user's goal.

In this paper, we introduce *DAUS*, a generative user simulator for TOD systems. As depicted in Figure 1, once initialized with the user goal description, *DAUS* engages with the system across multiple turns, providing information to fulfill the user's objectives. Our aim is to minimize the commonly observed user simulator hallucinations and incorrect responses (right-hand side of Figure 1), with an ultimate objective of enabling detection of common errors in TOD systems (left-hand side of Figure 1). Our approach is straightforward yet effective: we build upon the foundation of LLM-based simulators (Terragni et al., 2023; Owoicho et al., 2023) and extend such approach by fine-tuning the LLM on in-domain dialogues, annotated with their user goals. Notably, *DAUS* does not require insights into the inner-workings of the TOD system, its policy, nor system-specific functionalities, as it interacts with the TOD system strictly through natural language.



*Proceedings of the 1st Workshop on Simulating Conversational Intelligence in Chat (SCI-CHAT 2024)*, pages 19–35

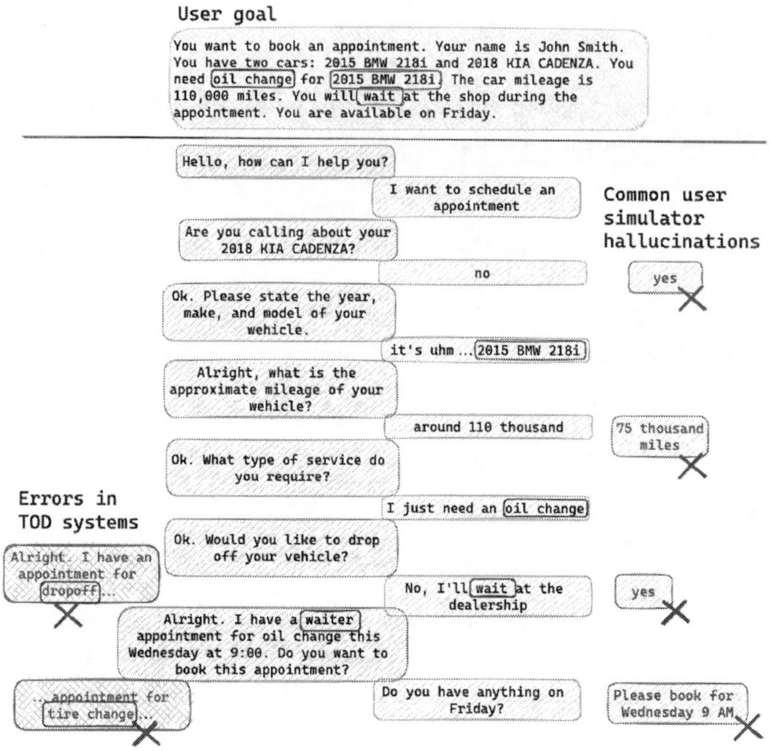


Figure 1: Example conversation between user simulator and TOD system. We aim to minimize common simulator's hallucinations (right) and thus ease the detection of TOD system failures (left).

We summarize our contributions and findings as follows:

- **Domain-Specific Adaptation**: *DAUS* fine-tunes a pre-trained LLM on domain-specific conversational data, enhancing the simulator's ability to maintain coherent and contextually relevant dialogues in a specific domain.

- **Reducing Simulator Hallucinations**: *DAUS* mitigates hallucinations originated from in-context learning approaches, which caused inconsistencies and irrelevant information in simulator responses. By fine-tuning on domain-specific data, our approach ensures more coherent and contextually relevant simulated dialogues.

- **Balancing Lexical Diversity in User Simulation**: *DAUS* employs LLMs for user simulation, offering a degree of lexical diversity in generated utterances. While not matching the diversity of in-context learning (partly due to hallucinations), it still provides language variety.

## 2 Related Work

### 2.1 Task-Oriented Dialogue Systems

The field of TOD systems, dedicated to interacting with users to accomplish specific tasks, has recently witnessed notable advancements (Zhang et al., 2020). Given the achievements of LLMs in various natural language processing tasks, there have been efforts to apply them to TOD systems (Raffel et al., 2020; Ouyang et al., 2022). A prominent application involves leveraging LLMs to extract users intents and entities, enhancing the Natural Language Understanding or Dialog State Tracking components (Zhao et al., 2022; Gupta et al., 2022b; Madotto et al., 2021; Madotto and Liu, 2020).

Furthermore, Hudeček and Dušek (2023) suggest that LLMs have the potential to be used off-the-shelf in TOD systems, even without fine-tuning for the specific TOD task, but their performance still lags behind supervised approaches. In response, an alternative approach underscores the benefits of fine-tuning specifically for TOD systems (Bang et al., 2023; Hosseini-Asl et al., 2020; Gupta et al., 2022a). This line of research reveals that fine-tune

LLMs can play a crucial role in enhancing the capabilities of TOD systems.

### 2.2 User Simulation

The state of the art in user simulation for TOD systems has evolved significantly in the recent years. Initially, Eckert et al. (1997) proposed the Bigram model, which estimates a user action conditioned on the system actions. Although efficient, this model does not account for the user goal coherence. Rule-based methods like Agenda-based (Schatzmann et al., 2007; Schatzmann and Young, 2009; Keizer et al., 2010) addresses the coherence issue but relies on the manual definition of rules.

Data-driven approaches, leveraging deep learning models (Gür et al., 2018; Asri et al., 2016; Lin et al., 2021, 2022, 2023), overcome the rule-based constraints but require significant computational resources and annotated data. These methods mandate dialog annotation for user goal fulfillment at each turn. In-context learning approaches (Terragni et al., 2023) have recently gained traction, designing prompts using snippets of example dialogues, the user's goal (expressed in natural language as in Terragni et al. (2023), or structured format as in Davidson et al. (2023)), and the dialog history. While these approaches demand fewer resources than fine-tuning methods and eschew manual annotation, they underscore limitations of LLMs, including hallucinations, repetitions, and incomplete user goal fulfillment.

## 3 Generative User Simulator

In this section, we define the task of generative user simulation for TOD systems. Moreover, we describe our approach, based on fine-tuned LLMs.

### 3.1 Background

When interacting with a TOD system, users aim to fulfill their goal, e.g., book a flight, or cancel their reservation in a restaurant. Therefore, a user simulator ($U$), designed to imitate a real user, interacts with the TOD system ($S$) with a given user goal $\mathcal{G}$. Formally, interactions are a sequence of utterances, where the system's utterances $s$ and the user's utterances $u$ take turns, forming a dialogue history $\mathcal{H} = [s_1, u_1, \ldots, s_t, u_t, \ldots, s_N, u_N]$, with $s_t$ and $u_t$ corresponding to system's and user's utterance at turn $t$, respectively, and $N$ being the total number of exchanged utterances.

We define the user goal $\mathcal{G}$ as all the information the user requires to achieve their aim. An example of user goal is the following: *You want to try an Indian restaurant. The restaurant must be cheap and in the center. Book a table for 2 people at 8PM*. At the end of the dialogue, we expect the user simulator to have fulfilled $\mathcal{G}$. While the goal $\mathcal{G}$ can be represented either in structural format (Davidson et al., 2023) or in natural language (Terragni et al., 2023), in this work we focus on $\mathcal{G}$ represented in natural language. $\mathcal{G}$ is usually defined by a domain expert or randomly sampled.

### 3.2 Our Approach

We propose Domain-Aware User Simulator (DAUS), a model that relies on learning the specifics of interactions with a TOD system from conversational data. The data needs to contain the goal $\mathcal{G}$ and the dialogue history $\mathcal{H}$. Typically, such datasets are derived from user conversations with production TOD systems, or created and curated through crowd-sourcing or user studies.

We cast the above-described problem of simulator's goal fulfillment to an utterance-level generation task. Specifically, the main task of $U$ is to generate the next utterance $u_t$ by modeling:

$$u_t = \phi(\mathcal{G}, \mathcal{H}) \quad (1)$$

where $\phi$ is the function to generate a user utterance. The $u_t$ needs be aligned with $\mathcal{G}$ and $\mathcal{H}$, i.e., it needs to be faithful towards the given goal, as well as coherent with the dialogue so far.

Given that both $\mathcal{G}$ and $\mathcal{H}$ are in natural language, we model $\phi$ from Eq. 1 with a language modeling-based approach. Specifically, we first construct a prompt to feed an LLM, by combining $\mathcal{G}$ and $\mathcal{H}$. We further employ the LLM to generate the $u_t$ in auto-regressive fashion:

$$p_{LLM}(\boldsymbol{u_t}|\mathcal{G}, \mathcal{H}) = \prod_{i=1}^{n} p_{LLM}(x_t^i|x_t^{<i}, \mathcal{G}, \mathcal{H}) \quad (2)$$

where $x_t^i$ is the $i$-th token of the utterance at turn $t$. We break down the dialogue from the data by turn, yielding $N$ data points for each conversation.

Regarding the interaction between our fine-tuned LLM and a TOD system, we follow the same paradigm from Terragni et al. (2023). *DAUS* receives a fresh prompt, which comprises the user's goal for the ongoing dialogue and the cumulative dialogue history. Unlike Terragni et al. (2023), we do not provide any example dialogues to serve as shots. We additionally post-process the generated utterance to ensure that a clean message is passed to TOD systems (i.e., removal of special characters and trailing tokens).

## 4 Experimental Setting

In this section, we describe datasets, implementation details, and experimental setting for simulator-system interactions.

### 4.1 Data sources

Table 1: Dataset Statistics (after pre-processing).

| Dataset | Avg # Turns | Avg # Words per User Utterance | Avg # Words per TOD Utterance |
|---|---|---|---|
| MultiWOZ | 5.86 | 13.13 | 14.86 |
| *AutomotiveData* | 11.20 | 3.44 | 12.06 |

We consider two data sources to evaluate our approach. First, we experiment on internal dialogue data of user-TOD system phone call interactions within the automotive industry, dubbed *AutomotiveData*.[1] Second, we use the well-established dataset of multi-domain TOD systems – MultiWOZ 2.1 (Eric et al., 2019). Both data sources contain user goal $\mathcal{G}$ in natural language and multi-turn dialogues (compliant with Section 3.1). For each dataset, we randomly sample 2,500 dialogues for training, 300 for testing and 300 for validation. The statistics of the resulting datasets are reported in Table 1.

### 4.2 TOD Systems

*DAUS* communicates with TOD systems through natural language, making it system-agnostic. For our user simulator fine-tuned on *AutomotiveData*, we employ an internal TOD system. To evaluate *DAUS* fine-tuned on MultiWOZ, we use the ConvLab2 framework (Zhu et al., 2020), extended by Terragni et al. (2023), which integrates LLM-based few-shot user simulators.[2] We use the same TOD the authors used in their original work. We identify a challenge with the default stopping criteria that prematurely end dialogues when users express gratitude. This does not always signify the end of the interaction as users may continue with their goals (e.g., *"Thanks for booking my flight. I also need a hotel"* would terminate the conversation). Therefore, we modify the criteria to exclude termination on *"thanks"* intent. We consequently re-run the experiments presented in Terragni et al. (2023). Moreover, we publicly release the updated framework and the user simulator fine-tuned on MultiWOZ 2.1 at `https://github.com/telepathylabsai/finetuned-user-simulator`.

### 4.3 User Goal Settings

For the MultiWOZ data within ConvLab2 framework, we follow the previous work for construction of the user goals (Zhu et al., 2020; Terragni et al., 2023). Specifically, the user goals are randomly sampled, conditioned on the domains and entities frequency in the training data. We generate 100 dialogues per user goal.

For evaluation on our internal TOD system, a domain expert manually defined user goals for 8 test cases, detailed in Appendix A. The test cases vary depending on the complexity and the main task that the simulator has to fulfill. As such, we label the test cases accordingly: *B* for *book* appointment task, *C* for *cancel* appointment task, *R* for *reschedule* appointment task. Moreover, each label is associated with a graded difficulty indicator, i.e., *easy* or *hard*. We generate 100 dialogues per test case (i.e., per user goal).

### 4.4 Fine-tuning Details

We conduct our experiments with the recently released open-source LLM — `Llama-2` (Touvron et al., 2023). The prompt, mentioned in Section 3.2, is constructed by concatenating the task description, user goal $\mathcal{G}$, and the dialog history $\mathcal{H}$. Moreover, we separate every utterance with a special "*<end-turn>*" token.

We utilize LoRA (Hu et al., 2021) – a parameter-efficient fine-tuning technique, capable of reaching performances comparable to fully fine-tuned models, whilst requiring only a fraction of the computational resources. We adhere to the hyperparameter recommendations and instructions of the recent work on the topic (Hu et al., 2021; He et al., 2021) and use the following LoRA hyperparameters throughout the experiments: rank $r$ of 64, $\alpha$ of 32, and dropout of 0.05. Moreover, we optimize attention layers (query and key matrices) of the `Llama-2` model. We use the 13B `Llama-2` ver-

[1] In order to protect our users' privacy, we do not release any user data nor models fine-tuned on user's data. Examples presented throughout the paper are synthetically constructed, whilst preserving realistic user goals. Users have been informed about and have consented to data collection.

[2] `https://github.com/telepathylabsai/prompt-based-user-simulator`.

sion for the main experiments, and the 7B version for comparison and the generalization study. We perform hyperparameter grid search for learning rate on the dev sets of our datasets. We settle for $lr = 3e^{-5}$ and the batch size of 12 and 32 for the 13B and 7B versions, respectively.

### 4.5 Baselines

We compare our Llama-2 fine-tuned model with several pre-trained models in zero-shot or few-shot fashion, following (Terragni et al., 2023; Davidson et al., 2023). In particular, we consider the following pre-trained models:

- Llama 2 with 13B parameters.
- GPT-3.5 Turbo4 (Chat-GPT), version 0613 (Brown et al., 2020a). For data privacy reasons, we employ this model only for the MultiWOZ experiments.
- Flan-T5 (Chung et al., 2022) with 3B parameters (XL), to reproduce results of Terragni et al. (2023).

In addition to the LLM-based models, we consider an agenda-based simulator (ABUS) (Wen et al., 2015), designed specifically for MultiWOZ within ConvLab2 framework, thus requiring the knowledge of TOD system's policy. We include two variants of `ABUS`: the first with template-based NLG and the second with data-driven NLG, dubbed `ABUS-T` and `ABUS-D`, respectively. Let us notice that ABUS is a strong baseline, as it is tailored for communicating with the MultiWOZ-based TOD from ConvLab2, therefore it is included as a reference of the potential upper-bound for user goal fulfillment performance. We follow Terragni et al. (2023) and set the temperature for inference to 0.9 for all MultiWOZ experiments, and 0.7 for internal experiments (value chosen through grid search).

## 5 Evaluation

We comprehensively evaluate our method, aiming to assess its ability to achieve designated user goals in dialogues and its impact on lexical diversity when aligning with real user language patterns. Moreover, we perform qualitative analysis of simulated dialogues via human evaluation. In this section, we detail these evaluation procedures.

Additionally, we examine utterance-level metrics, comparing generated utterances with those in the target dataset, using both general natural language generation and domain-specific entity-based metrics. However, we found that these metrics poorly correlate with the simulator's task completion. Detailed information about these metrics and their results can be found in Appendix C.

### 5.1 Goal Fulfillment Evaluation Metrics

Our objective is to evaluate the goal fulfillment at the end of the dialogue. For MultiWOZ experiments, we consider well-known metrics such as Success, Completion and Book rate. These metrics aim to capture how successful was the dialogue in terms of fulfilling specific subtasks from the user goal (e.g., whether the restaurant is booked). We also compute the average precision ($P$), recall ($R$) and $F_1$ scores by matching the entities expressed through the simulated dialogue to the ones in the initial user goal. These metrics aim to assess the simulator's faithfulness and consistency of entities with the user goal (e.g., whether the correct restaurant *type* was booked). For a comprehensive understanding of the metric definitions, please refer to Zhu et al. (2020) and Terragni et al. (2023).

Regarding our in-house TOD, it is worth noting that we do not differentiate between *book*, *inform* and *request* entities. Therefore, we adapt the mentioned metrics, except for the Book Rate, while considering all entities as inform entities. Moreover, we compute several metrics specific to automotive domain: *user subtask* indicating whether the subtask (*book*, *cancel*, or *reschedule* the appointment) matches the one given in the user goal; *caller info* and *car info* indicating whether user information (name, phone number) and vehicle information (car year, make, and model) match the ones in the goal, respectively; *transport type* assessing the chosen transport type (e.g., dropping of the vehicle, waiting for the service in the dealership).

### 5.2 Lexical Diversity of Generated Utterances

Lexical diversity (LD) is a measure of word variability and vocabulary size of a given text corpus, in our case, the set of generated user utterances from 100 conversations. We report MTLD scores (McCarthy, 2005), and a number of unigram words (Unig) and average user utterance length (UttLen). LD results are reported in Section 6.2.

### 5.3 Qualitative Analysis

During the analysis of the generated simulated dialogues, we observed several re-occurring issues. We categorize them as the simulator's failure (*hallucination*, *incomplete user goal* fulfillment, or *loop-*

Table 2: Results of goal fulfillment task in simulator interaction with the internal TOD system. The results are averaged across the eight user goals.

| Model | Num Shots | Compl Rate | Succ Rate | $P$ | $R$ | $F_1$ | User Subtask | Caller Info | Car Info | Transport Type | UttLen | Unig | MTLD |
|---|---|---|---|---|---|---|---|---|---|---|---|---|---|
| FlanT5-XL (Terragni et al., 2023) | 2 | 0.46 | 0.27 | 0.72 | 0.86 | 0.76 | 70.9 | 85.5 | 65.6 | 39.2 | **2.8** | **209** | **23.4** |
| Llama-2 | 0 | 0.35 | 0.13 | 0.62 | 0.87 | 0.69 | 50.4 | 88.8 | 72.2 | 12.8 | 2.4 | 161 | 15.5 |
| | 1 | 0.37 | 0.12 | 0.67 | 0.89 | 0.74 | 65.6 | 89.1 | 81.6 | 8.0 | 2.0 | 149 | 14.5 |
| | 2 | 0.36 | 0.15 | 0.66 | 0.91 | 0.74 | 68.9 | 90.3 | 80.2 | 8.0 | 2.0 | 129 | 13.7 |
| *DAUS* | 0 | **0.51** | **0.40** | **0.91** | **0.92** | **0.91** | **99.5** | **98.5** | **99.0** | **80.7** | 1.7 | 112 | 16.5 |

*ing/repeating* utterances across turns) or TOD system's failure (*NLU misclassification* due to missing user's intent or entities, *forcing end of dialogue*, or *looping/repeating* utterances). Our aim is to assess the prevalence of these patterns and identify potential limitations of LLM-based user simulators. To this end, we employ three annotators to annotate 45 dialogues generated with an LLM-based baseline and 45 dialogues generated with *DAUS* within ConvLab2 framework. The annotators are domain-experts and employees of the authors' institution. We provide guidelines for each of the categories and go through an on-boarding process with the annotators. The labels for each of the dialogues are determined by majority vote. Annotators reach moderate to good agreement, as measured by Fleiss' $\kappa$, detailed in Appendix D.

## 6 Results

In this section, we examine our study's findings across three main threads. First, we investigate the impact of fine-tuning LLMs with domain-specific data on goal fulfillment in dialog interactions (Section 6.1). Next, we explore the link between fine-tuning and the lexical diversity of generated utterances (Section 6.2). Finally, we assess whether the adaptability of LLM-based user simulators to unseen user tasks is influenced by the diversity of subtask types in their training data (Section 6.3).

### 6.1 Goal Fulfillment

**Internal TOD System.** Table 2 shows results on the goal fulfillment task of *DAUS* and the baselines detailed in Section 4.5, averaged across different user goals. We present the results per each of the eight specific user goals, detailed in Section 4.3, in Appendix B for space-saving purposes.

As a first remark, *DAUS* outperforms all of the baselines across all the goal fulfillment metrics. We observe the largest improvements for domain-specific metrics, e.g., precision and recall of relevant entities and accuracy of the transport type. This indicates that fine-tuning on in-domain data improves simulator's knowledge of the domain-specific terminology. We further expand on this observation in Section 7.1.

Regarding the baselines, `FlanT5`, employing 2 shots as examples, is the second best model. As observed in (Terragni et al., 2023) as well, this instruction fine-tuned model outperforms `Llama-2` with 2 shots in most of the cases.

**MultiWOZ Data within ConvLab2.** We show the goal fulfillment performance of *DAUS* and the baselines in interaction with ConvLab2's TOD system on MultiWOZ 2.1 in Table 3. As in Section 6.1, we observe strong performance of *DAUS*. Specifically, *DAUS* outperforms all of the in-context learning approaches in terms of goal fulfillment, including prior state-of-the-art (Terragni et al., 2023). Moreover, our method outperforms few-shot `GPT-3.5`, a model significantly larger than ours (estimated 175 billion parameters vs 13 billion). This further suggests the benefits of fine-tuning LLMs on domain-specific conversational data, as stronger performance can be achieved with significantly smaller LLMs, thus reducing the computational requirements of the simulator.

As a general remark, results on both benchmarks, i.e., the ConvLab2 and our internal one, show significant improvements across multiple goal fulfillment metrics. Thus, we conclude that *DAUS* indeed does lead to more consistent, reliable, and faithful LLM-based user simulators. We will discuss these results more in depth in our qualitative analysis in Section 7.1.

### 6.2 Lexical Diversity

Lexical diversity (LD) of generated user utterances from internal TOD system and MultiWOZ experiments is presented in the last 3 columns of Tables 2

Table 3: Performance on MultiWOZ 2.1 within ConvLab2 framework.

| Model | Num Shots | Compl Rate | Succ Rate | Book Rate | $P$ | $R$ | $F_1$ | UttLen | Unig | MTLD |
|---|---|---|---|---|---|---|---|---|---|---|
| ABUS-T (Wen et al., 2015) | - | 0.93 | 0.83 | 0.85 | 0.84 | 0.94 | 0.86 | **17.4** | 527 | 46.9 |
| ABUS-D (Wen et al., 2015) | - | 0.86 | 0.60 | 0.75 | 0.87 | 0.90 | 0.87 | 9.8 | 327 | 28.0 |
| FlanT5-XL (Terragni et al., 2023) | 2 | 0.19 | 0.13 | 0.46 | 0.45 | 0.39 | 0.39 | 13.7 | **888** | 41.2 |
| Llama-2 | 0 | 0.07 | 0.04 | 0.13 | 0.31 | 0.21 | 0.23 | 8.1 | 697 | 30.7 |
| | 2 | 0.09 | 0.08 | 0.30 | 0.46 | 0.34 | 0.39 | 10.0 | 765 | 38.8 |
| GPT-3.5 | 2 | 0.35 | 0.19 | 0.34 | 0.49 | 0.52 | 0.48 | 16.3 | 626 | 38.1 |
| *DAUS* | 0 | **0.41** | **0.29** | **0.66** | **0.69** | **0.69** | **0.67** | 10.6 | 789 | **54.9** |

and 3. We observe a drop in LD, as measured by the length of the generated utterances and the total number of unigrams, when *DAUS* is fine-tuned on *AutomotiveData*. This suggests a limited vocabulary in the training data, which is expected due to the real users often responding with one or two words, especially in the *cancel* task. *DAUS* had a relatively high MTLD score, because of the correctly generated caller, car and transport entities, which usually have unique values. However, a low unigram score is due to averaging metrics over 8 user tasks, where only 3 of them are the entity-rich *book* task. Meanwhile, the higher LD of FlanT5-based method is due to its prevalent hallucinations, thus falsely inflating the LD scores by generating out-of-context content (see Section 7.1).

In MultiWOZ-based experiments, results indicate higher LD than ABUS baselines, as measured by MTLD, while the generated utterances are slightly shorter compared to FlanT5. As such, *DAUS* does not seem to lose LD during fine-tuning on MultiWOZ, while fine-tuning on *AutomotiveData* seems to reduce it slightly. This can be explained by the fact that *AutomotiveData* contains both specific vocabulary and utterances from real product users, which makes it hard for in-context learning approaches to imitate. On the other hand, fine-tuning procedure enables the model to learn the particulars of such interactions.

### 6.3 Generalization to Unseen User Tasks

Table 4 shows the percentage of successful subtask identifications for four variants of our model: *DAUS* fine-tuned on the full dataset described in Section 4.1, and *DAUS* fine-tuned on modified datasets by removing certain subtasks (*book (B)*, *cancel (C)*, or *reschedule (R)*) from the training sets. With this experiment, we aim to assess the generalization abilities of our approach.

Table 4: Percentage of dialogues with successfully identified subtask types across the test cases, with models fine-tuned on specific combinations of subtask types.

| | *DAUS (C+R+B)* | *C+R* | *B+R* | *B+C* |
|---|---|---|---|---|
| $B_{easy}$ | 99 | 100 | 100 | 99 |
| $B_{hard1}$ | 93 | 29 | 85 | 99 |
| $B_{hard2}$ | 99 | 86 | 94 | 97 |
| $C_{easy}$ | 96 | 100 | 75 | 99 |
| $C_{hard}$ | 100 | 100 | 77 | 96 |
| $R_{easy}$ | 88 | 100 | 98 | 34 |
| $R_{hard1}$ | 97 | 50 | 69 | 0 |
| $R_{hard2}$ | 86 | 84 | 56 | 0 |

Results show a decrease in performance when a model is not shown the specific subtask during training. For example, when we fine-tune *DAUS* on the combination of *book* and *reschedule* subtasks, we observe a considerable drop in performance on the *cancel* subtask. However, the largest drop is observed in the most complex subtask type, *reschedule*, where the model fine-tuned on *B+C* data completely fails to successfully communicate its goal for both $R_{hard}$ test cases.

We can conclude that *DAUS* does not generalize well to unseen user goal subtasks. Nevertheless, the overall performance of the fine-tuned models across all of the subtasks is still comparable to the performance of few-shot based models (e.g., *B+C* correctly predicts the subtask type, on average, in 66% of the dialogues, while Llama-2 2-shot does it in 69% of the dialogues, on average).

## 7 Qualitative Analysis

In this section, we detail and discuss the findings of our qualitative analysis of simulated dialogues.

Table 5: Percentage of the observed patterns per sample annotated in simulated dialogues in MultiWOZ.

| Label | *FlanT5* | *DAUS* |
|---|---|---|
| Hallucination | 73% | 36% |
| Looping simulator | 69% | 6% |
| Incomplete goal | 78% | 53% |
| Looping system | 20% | 22% |
| NLU misclassification | 60% | 40% |
| Forced end | 27% | 27% |

### 7.1 Human Evaluation of Generated Dialogues

Table 5 presents the prevalence of patterns, described in Section 5.3, observed through manual annotation of the simulated MultiWOZ dialogues. We observe consistent decrease in hallucinations, reduced number of dialogues with incomplete goal fulfillment, as well as reduced repetition of utterances in dialogues generated by *DAUS*, compared to `FlanT5`-based simulator. Below, we report the main findings from our analysis.

**Hallucinations.** The percentage of dialogues containing hallucinations drops from 73% for `FlanT5`-based simulator to 36% with *DAUS*. We observe that `FlanT5` frequently experiences severe failures, mostly because it generates non-specified pieces of information, such as defining a random range of time for a taxi pickup, inventing a location for an attraction or referring to a restaurant that have not been previously mentioned. Such hallucinations lead to dialogue failures, without possibility to recover the conversation. On the other hand, *DAUS* does not hallucinate nor misinterpret entities from the user goal and the dialogue, but rather sometimes asks for additional information that is not required by the user goal (e.g., asking restaurant's phone number, even though it is not strictly specified in the goal). Thus, we conclude that not only the prevalence of the hallucinations is reduced, but also their severity.

**TOD system failures.** We observe that the dialogue frequently stops before all of the subtasks from the user goal are completed (i.e., if the goal requires to book a restaurant and a taxi, perhaps only the restaurant is booked). While this is partly due to the simulator missing certain part of the user goal, it often happens due to the TOD system failures. We observe several issues with the TOD system within the ConvLab2 framework. First, as mentioned in the previous paragraph, the system aims to prematurely complete the dialogue, thus offering no opportunity to the user (simulator) to fully express their goal. Second, the system's NLU component often misclassifies certain entities, leading to incorrectly booked restaurants or similar. An example dialogue of both prematurely ending the dialogue and NLU misclassification:

*CUSTOMER: Can you help me with a robbery that happened? I am the victim.*
*ASSISTANT: Thank you for using our services .* ***(forcing premature end of conversation)***
*CUSTOMER: It happened at 9:10*
*ASSISTANT: Can you tell me which day you 'd like to travel on? What is your destination? Where will you be departing from?* ***(NLU misclassification)***

Finally, we observe loops in system's policy, where the system is stuck in policy states and is not able to continue the conversation.

### 7.2 Domain-specific Vocabulary

During our analysis of conversations generated using our internal TOD system, we observed that *DAUS* acquires domain-specific vocabulary, which we believe enhances its performance. For instance, when scheduling a vehicle service appointment, customers specify the preferred transport type, usually *dropoff* (the customer drops off the vehicle and returns when the service is complete) or *waiter* (the customer waits at the dealership during the service). This phenomenon, supported by performance improvements for *Transport Type* (see Table 2), is evident through qualitative dialogue analysis. Our initial experiments indicate that in-context learning approaches aiming to explain these terms in the prompt do not consistently capture their nuances.

Additionally, we noticed that, when fine-tuned on *AutomotiveData* containing phone call conversations with real users, *DAUS* tends to generate filler words like "uhm" and "yeah".

## 8 Conclusions

The use of a domain-aware LLM-based user simulator, such as *DAUS*, shows promising results in multi-turn interactions with TOD systems. *DAUS* can fulfill user goals by generating consistent and faithful utterances. Compared to previous LLM-based approaches (Terragni et al., 2023), our method has demonstrated superior performance, as measured by multiple metrics designed to capture the fulfillment of the given goal, as well as faithfulness across the dialogue. This indicates that *DAUS* is capable of effectively simulating user behavior and can serve as a valuable tool for testing and evaluating TOD systems. Moreover, our approach requires relatively small training dataset and imposes modest computational demands, thanks to parameter-efficient fine-tuning. This discovery aligns with findings in related research that contrasts in-context learning with parameter-efficient fine-tuning (Mosbach et al., 2023; Liu et al., 2022). Consequently, our approach emerges as a pragmatic choice for broader adoption within the NLP and Conversational AI community.

The potential applications of LLM-based user simulators are synthetic data augmentation (Li et al., 2022), supporting reinforcement learning approaches (Shi et al., 2019), and TOD system evaluation (Terragni et al., 2023; Zhu et al., 2020). *DAUS*'s reliability and consistency to the user goal make it particularly suitable for TOD system evaluation. As we have seen previously, an incomplete user goal can mainly imply two scenarios: a user simulator who hallucinates or a TOD system that is not able to understand the user's requirements. Therefore, the presence of a reliable user simulator is crucial: it allows us to identify the TOD system's errors with high accuracy.

Moreover, we stress that at the center of our approach is an LLM, leading to potentially different generations given the same input, depending on the sampling method. This means that *DAUS* is more flexible than certain agenda-based simulators, which usually rely on template-based responses. As such, we are able to simulate a dialogue with the same user goal multiple times, which results in multiple different attempts of the simulator to fulfill its goal, going through potentially different conversational paths. Therefore, we are able to test the robustness of the TOD system to different expressions of the same user goal.

## 9 Limitations

The approach employed in our study has several inherent limitations, primarily stemming from the use of LLMs. Most notably, GPT-3.5, the model we utilized in our experiments, is not open-source and freely available, which can hinder replicability of the experiments. Another limitation is related to the opaqueness of the model's training and fine-tuning processes. These models undergo pre-training and fine-tuning on diverse datasets, the specifics of which are often undisclosed. Consequently, it is challenging to ascertain whether these models have been exposed to specific datasets, such as MultiWOZ 2.1, or datasets with similar characteristics, which could raise concerns about models performance and potential biases.

Furthermore, our experiments were conducted exclusively on two English-language datasets. While LLMs are known for their transfer learning capabilities, allowing for the potential extension of results to other datasets, there is no guarantee of their generalizability across various domains or low-resource languages. The effectiveness of these models in domains distinct from the ones they were trained on remains uncertain and should be approached with caution.

In our analysis, we also observed instances where LLMs exhibit hallucinations. Despite being superior to in-context learning approaches like (Terragni et al., 2023), we still encountered cases of LLM responses that deviated from the expected or coherent output. These hallucinations may lead to unpredictable and potentially inappropriate responses in certain conversational contexts, raising concerns about the reliability and safety of such systems.

We also noticed a decrease in performance when certain user subtasks are omitted from the training dataset when we fine-tune *DAUS*, although the overall performance remains comparable to that of few-shot models. In our analysis, we did not investigate if providing one or two dialog shots would address this performance decrease.

Finally, the methodology relies on conversational data for fine-tuning LLMs. This reliance introduces additional limitations. Firstly, obtaining suitable conversational data may be challenging or even unfeasible in some scenarios. Researchers may resort to crowd-sourcing tools to gather dialogue examples or use LLMs themselves to generate synthetic data, which could introduce biases or inaccuracies. Secondly, the quality of the conversational data used for fine-tuning plays a pivotal role in the model's performance. In our study, we utilized well-curated conversational data, but we did not investigate the impact of using noisier or less meticulously curated data. The use of lower-quality data sources may affect the model's performance and raise questions about its reliability and robustness in real-world applications.

## 10 Ethics Statement

The use of LLMs for user simulation raises ethical considerations. We acknowledge the potential for perpetuating biases and stereotypes present in the data used to train these models (Brown et al., 2020b; Lucy and Bamman, 2021; Bender et al., 2021). While we have not implemented specific measures to mitigate these risks in this paper, we recognize their importance and urge the research community to address these challenges.

It is essential to note that we have used the user simulator solely to evaluate the performance of a dialogue system. However, LLMs can be used in a reinforcement learning setting to train dialog systems (Shi et al., 2019). In such cases, it is crucial to use these models judiciously because of their unpredictable and potentially inappropriate responses.

In addition to ethical considerations, it is crucial to acknowledge the significant environmental impact of LLMs. Their training and deployment consumes a considerable amount of energy, leading to environmental issues (Strubell et al., 2019). We should also be aware of the significant carbon footprint while fine-tuning the LLMs and using them for inference.

## Acknowledgement

Our gratitude to Damián Pascual for streamlining the implementation of the fine-tuning framework, saving us valuable time. Special thanks to the reviewers, Diana Nicoleta Popa, Vijeta Avijeet, and our colleagues at Telepathy Labs in Zürich for their constructive feedback and insightful discussions.

## References

Layla El Asri, Jing He, and Kaheer Suleman. 2016. A sequence-to-sequence model for user simulation in spoken dialogue systems. In *Interspeech 2016, 17th Annual Conference of the International Speech Communication Association*, pages 1151–1155. ISCA.

Krisztian Balog and ChengXiang Zhai. 2023. User simulation for evaluating information access systems. *arXiv preprint arXiv:2306.08550*.

Namo Bang, Jeehyun Lee, and Myoung-Wan Koo. 2023. Task-optimized adapters for an end-to-end task-oriented dialogue system. *arXiv preprint arXiv:2305.02468*.

Emily M Bender, Timnit Gebru, Angelina McMillan-Major, and Shmargaret Shmitchell. 2021. On the dangers of stochastic parrots: Can language models be too big? In *Proceedings of the 2021 ACM conference on fairness, accountability, and transparency*, pages 610–623.

Tom Brown, Benjamin Mann, Nick Ryder, Melanie Subbiah, Jared D Kaplan, Prafulla Dhariwal, Arvind Neelakantan, Pranav Shyam, Girish Sastry, Amanda Askell, et al. 2020a. Language models are few-shot learners. *Advances in neural information processing systems*, 33:1877–1901.

Tom B. Brown, Benjamin Mann, Nick Ryder, Melanie Subbiah, Jared Kaplan, Prafulla Dhariwal, Arvind Neelakantan, Pranav Shyam, Girish Sastry, Amanda Askell, Sandhini Agarwal, Ariel Herbert-Voss, Gretchen Krueger, Tom Henighan, Rewon Child, Aditya Ramesh, Daniel M. Ziegler, Jeffrey Wu, Clemens Winter, Christopher Hesse, Mark Chen, Eric Sigler, Mateusz Litwin, Scott Gray, Benjamin Chess, Jack Clark, Christopher Berner, Sam McCandlish, Alec Radford, Ilya Sutskever, and Dario Amodei. 2020b. Language models are few-shot learners. *Advances in neural information processing systems*, 33:1877–1901.

Hyung Won Chung, Le Hou, Shayne Longpre, Barret Zoph, Yi Tay, William Fedus, Eric Li, Xuezhi Wang, Mostafa Dehghani, Siddhartha Brahma, et al. 2022. Scaling instruction-finetuned language models. *arXiv preprint arXiv:2210.11416*.

Sam Davidson, Salvatore Romeo, Raphael Shu, James Gung, Arshit Gupta, Saab Mansour, and Yi Zhang. 2023. User simulation with large language models for evaluating task-oriented dialogue. *arXiv preprint arXiv:2309.13233*.

Wieland Eckert, Esther Levin, and Roberto Pieraccini. 1997. User modeling for spoken dialogue system evaluation. *1997 IEEE Workshop on Automatic Speech Recognition and Understanding Proceedings*, pages 80–87.

Mihail Eric, Rahul Goel, Shachi Paul, Abhishek Sethi, Sanchit Agarwal, Shuyag Gao, and Dilek Hakkani-Tur. 2019. Multiwoz 2.1: Multi-domain dialogue state corrections and state tracking baselines. *arXiv preprint arXiv:1907.01669*.

Prakhar Gupta, Cathy Jiao, Yi-Ting Yeh, Shikib Mehri, Maxine Eskenazi, and Jeffrey Bigham. 2022a. InstructDial: Improving zero and few-shot generalization in dialogue through instruction tuning. In *Proceedings of the 2022 Conference on Empirical Methods in Natural Language Processing*, pages 505–525, Abu Dhabi, United Arab Emirates. Association for Computational Linguistics.

Raghav Gupta, Harrison Lee, Jeffrey Zhao, Yuan Cao, Abhinav Rastogi, and Yonghui Wu. 2022b. Show, don't tell: Demonstrations outperform descriptions for schema-guided task-oriented dialogue. In *Proceedings of the 2022 Conference of the North American Chapter of the Association for Computational Linguistics: Human Language Technologies*, pages

4541–4549, Seattle, United States. Association for Computational Linguistics.

Izzeddin Gür, Dilek Hakkani-Tür, Gokhan Tür, and Pararth Shah. 2018. User modeling for task oriented dialogues. In *2018 IEEE Spoken Language Technology Workshop (SLT)*, pages 900–906. IEEE.

Junxian He, Chunting Zhou, Xuezhe Ma, Taylor Berg-Kirkpatrick, and Graham Neubig. 2021. Towards a unified view of parameter-efficient transfer learning. *arXiv preprint arXiv:2110.04366*.

Ehsan Hosseini-Asl, Bryan McCann, Chien-Sheng Wu, Semih Yavuz, and Richard Socher. 2020. A simple language model for task-oriented dialogue. *Advances in Neural Information Processing Systems*, 33:20179–20191.

Edward J Hu, Yelong Shen, Phillip Wallis, Zeyuan Allen-Zhu, Yuanzhi Li, Shean Wang, Lu Wang, and Weizhu Chen. 2021. Lora: Low-rank adaptation of large language models. *arXiv preprint arXiv:2106.09685*.

Vojtěch Hudeček and Ondřej Dušek. 2023. Are llms all you need for task-oriented dialogue? *arXiv preprint arXiv:2304.06556*.

Tianbo Ji, Yvette Graham, Gareth Jones, Chenyang Lyu, and Qun Liu. 2022. Achieving reliable human assessment of open-domain dialogue systems. In *Proceedings of the 60th Annual Meeting of the Association for Computational Linguistics (Volume 1: Long Papers)*, ACL'22, pages 6416–6437.

Ziwei Ji, Nayeon Lee, Rita Frieske, Tiezheng Yu, Dan Su, Yan Xu, Etsuko Ishii, Ye Jin Bang, Andrea Madotto, and Pascale Fung. 2023. Survey of hallucination in natural language generation. *ACM Comput. Surv.*, 55(12).

Simon Keizer, Milica Gasic, Filip Jurcicek, François Mairesse, Blaise Thomson, Kai Yu, and Steve Young. 2010. Parameter estimation for agenda-based user simulation. In *Proceedings of the SIGDIAL 2010 Conference*, pages 116–123.

Alon Lavie and Abhaya Agarwal. 2007. Meteor: An automatic metric for mt evaluation with high levels of correlation with human judgments. In *Proceedings of the Second Workshop on Statistical Machine Translation*, StatMT '07, page 228–231, USA. Association for Computational Linguistics.

Xiujun Li, Zachary C Lipton, Bhuwan Dhingra, Lihong Li, Jianfeng Gao, and Yun-Nung Chen. 2016. A user simulator for task-completion dialogues. *arXiv preprint arXiv:1612.05688*.

Zekun Li, Wenhu Chen, Shiyang Li, Hong Wang, Jing Qian, and Xifeng Yan. 2022. Controllable Dialogue Simulation with In-context Learning. In *Findings of the Association for Computational Linguistics: EMNLP 2022*, pages 4330–4347. Association for Computational Linguistics.

Chin-Yew Lin. 2004. Rouge: A package for automatic evaluation of summaries. In *Text summarization branches out*, pages 74–81.

Hsien-Chin Lin, Shutong Feng, Christian Geishauser, Nurul Lubis, Carel van Niekerk, Michael Heck, Benjamin Ruppik, Renato Vukovic, and Milica Gasić. 2023. Emous: Simulating user emotions in task-oriented dialogues. In *Proceedings of the 46th International ACM SIGIR Conference on Research and Development in Information Retrieval*, pages 2526–2531.

Hsien-Chin Lin, Christian Geishauser, Shutong Feng, Nurul Lubis, Carel van Niekerk, Michael Heck, and Milica Gasic. 2022. GenTUS: Simulating User Behaviour and Language in Task-oriented Dialogues with Generative Transformers. In *Proceedings of the 23rd Annual Meeting of the Special Interest Group on Discourse and Dialogue, SIGDIAL 2022,*, pages 270–282. Association for Computational Linguistics.

Hsien-Chin Lin, Nurul Lubis, Songbo Hu, Carel van Niekerk, Christian Geishauser, Michael Heck, Shutong Feng, and Milica Gasic. 2021. Domain-independent User Simulation with Transformers for Task-oriented Dialogue Systems. In *Proceedings of the 22nd Annual Meeting of the Special Interest Group on Discourse and Dialogue, SIGdial 2021*, pages 445–456. Association for Computational Linguistics.

Haokun Liu, Derek Tam, Mohammed Muqeeth, Jay Mohta, Tenghao Huang, Mohit Bansal, and Colin A Raffel. 2022. Few-shot parameter-efficient fine-tuning is better and cheaper than in-context learning. *Advances in Neural Information Processing Systems*, 35:1950–1965.

Li Lucy and David Bamman. 2021. Gender and representation bias in gpt-3 generated stories. In *Proceedings of the Third Workshop on Narrative Understanding*, pages 48–55.

Andrea Madotto, Zhaojiang Lin, Genta Indra Winata, and Pascale Fung. 2021. Few-shot bot: Prompt-based learning for dialogue systems. *arXiv preprint arXiv:2110.08118*.

Andrea Madotto and Zihan Liu. 2020. Language models as few-shot learner for task-oriented dialogue systems. *ArXiv*, abs/2008.06239.

Philip M McCarthy. 2005. *An assessment of the range and usefulness of lexical diversity measures and the potential of the measure of textual, lexical diversity (MTLD)*. Ph.D. thesis, The University of Memphis.

Marius Mosbach, Tiago Pimentel, Shauli Ravfogel, Dietrich Klakow, and Yanai Elazar. 2023. Few-shot fine-tuning vs. in-context learning: A fair comparison and evaluation. In *Findings of the Association for Computational Linguistics: ACL 2023*, pages 12284–12314, Toronto, Canada. Association for Computational Linguistics.

Long Ouyang, Jeff Wu, Xu Jiang, Diogo Almeida, Carroll L. Wainwright, Pamela Mishkin, Chong Zhang, Sandhini Agarwal, Katarina Slama, Alex Ray, John Schulman, Jacob Hilton, Fraser Kelton, Luke Miller, Maddie Simens, Amanda Askell, Peter Welinder, Paul Christiano, Jan Leike, and Ryan Lowe. 2022. Training language models to follow instructions with human feedback.

Paul Owoicho, Ivan Sekulic, Mohammad Aliannejadi, Jeffrey Dalton, and Fabio Crestani. 2023. Exploiting simulated user feedback for conversational search: Ranking, rewriting, and beyond. In *Proceedings of the 46th International ACM SIGIR Conference on Research and Development in Information Retrieval*, pages 632–642.

Kishore Papineni, Salim Roukos, Todd Ward, and Wei-Jing Zhu. 2002. Bleu: a method for automatic evaluation of machine translation. In *Proceedings of the 40th annual meeting of the Association for Computational Linguistics*, pages 311–318.

Colin Raffel, Noam Shazeer, Adam Roberts, Katherine Lee, Sharan Narang, Michael Matena, Yanqi Zhou, Wei Li, and Peter J. Liu. 2020. Exploring the limits of transfer learning with a unified text-to-text transformer. *J. Mach. Learn. Res.*, 21(1).

Jost Schatzmann, Blaise Thomson, Karl Weilhammer, Hui Ye, and Steve Young. 2007. Agenda-based user simulation for bootstrapping a pomdp dialogue system. In *Human Language Technologies 2007: The Conference of the North American Chapter of the Association for Computational Linguistics; Companion Volume, Short Papers*, pages 149–152.

Jost Schatzmann and Steve J. Young. 2009. The hidden agenda user simulation model. *IEEE Transactions on Audio, Speech, and Language Processing*, 17:733–747.

Ivan Sekulić, Mohammad Aliannejadi, and Fabio Crestani. 2022. Evaluating mixed-initiative conversational search systems via user simulation. In *Proceedings of the Fifteenth ACM International Conference on Web Search and Data Mining*, pages 888–896.

Weiyan Shi, Kun Qian, Xuewei Wang, and Zhou Yu. 2019. How to build user simulators to train rl-based dialog systems. In *Proceedings of the 2019 Conference on Empirical Methods in Natural Language Processing and the 9th International Joint Conference on Natural Language Processing (EMNLP-IJCNLP)*, pages 1990–2000.

Emma Strubell, Ananya Ganesh, and Andrew McCallum. 2019. Energy and policy considerations for deep learning in nlp. In *Proceedings of the 57th Annual Meeting of the Association for Computational Linguistics*, pages 3645–3650.

Silvia Terragni, Modestas Filipavicius, Nghia Khau, Bruna Guedes, André Manso, and Roland Mathis. 2023. In-context learning user simulators for task-oriented dialog systems. In *Proceedings of the 1st Workshop on Foundations and Applications in Large-scale AI Models -Pre-training, Fine-tuning, and Prompt-based Learning*.

Hugo Touvron, Louis Martin, Kevin Stone, Peter Albert, Amjad Almahairi, Yasmine Babaei, Nikolay Bashlykov, Soumya Batra, Prajjwal Bhargava, Shruti Bhosale, et al. 2023. Llama 2: Open foundation and fine-tuned chat models. *arXiv preprint arXiv:2307.09288*.

Dazhen Wan, Zheng Zhang, Qi Zhu, Lizi Liao, and Minlie Huang. 2022. A unified dialogue user simulator for few-shot data augmentation. In *Findings of the Association for Computational Linguistics: EMNLP 2022*, pages 3788–3799, Abu Dhabi, United Arab Emirates. Association for Computational Linguistics.

Tsung-Hsien Wen, Milica Gašić, Nikola Mrkšić, Pei-Hao Su, David Vandyke, and Steve Young. 2015. Semantically conditioned LSTM-based natural language generation for spoken dialogue systems. In *Proceedings of the 2015 Conference on Empirical Methods in Natural Language Processing*, pages 1711–1721. Association for Computational Linguistics.

Tianyi Zhang, Varsha Kishore, Felix Wu, Kilian Q Weinberger, and Yoav Artzi. 2019. Bertscore: Evaluating text generation with bert. *arXiv preprint arXiv:1904.09675*.

Zheng Zhang, Ryuichi Takanobu, Qi Zhu, MinLie Huang, and XiaoYan Zhu. 2020. Recent advances and challenges in task-oriented dialog systems. *Science China Technological Sciences*, 63(10):2011–2027.

Jeffrey Zhao, Raghav Gupta, Yuan Cao, Dian Yu, Mingqiu Wang, Harrison Lee, Abhinav Rastogi, Izhak Shafran, and Yonghui Wu. 2022. Description-driven task-oriented dialog modeling. *arXiv preprint arXiv:2201.08904*.

Qi Zhu, Zheng Zhang, Yan Fang, Xiang Li, Ryuichi Takanobu, Jinchao Li, Baolin Peng, Jianfeng Gao, Xiaoyan Zhu, and Minlie Huang. 2020. Convlab-2: An open-source toolkit for building, evaluating, and diagnosing dialogue systems. In *Proceedings of the 58th Annual Meeting of the Association for Computational Linguistics*.

## A User tasks

Description of eight different test cases (user goals) are provided in Table 6. We additionally add comparisons with `FlanT5-XXL`.

Table 6: Description of user goals with subtask types.

| # | User subtask | Difficulty | User goal details |
|---|---|---|---|
| 1 | Book | Easy | New customer; Available: today 4PM; Transport_type: waiter; Service: check engine. |
| 2 | Book | Hard | Known customer with 1 appointment and 2 cars; Available: Wednesday; Transport_type: dropoff; Unknown Service. |
| 3 | Book | Hard | Known customer with 3 appointments and 2 cars; Available: Wednesday; Transport_type: dropoff; Two services: engine overheating and oil change. |
| 4 | Cancel | Easy | Known customer with 1 appointment. |
| 5 | Cancel | Hard | Known customer with 3 appointments. |
| 6 | Reschedule | Easy | Known customer with 1 appointment; Available: 10 AM; Transport_type: dropoff; Unknown service. |
| 7 | Reschedule | Hard | Known customer with 1 appointment; Available: afternoon; Transport_type: waiter; Service: oil change. |
| 8 | Reschedule | Hard | Known customer from unknown phone number; With 3 appointments; Available: Wednesday; Transport_type: loaner; Two services: Oil change and engine check |

## B Results per Tasks

Table 8 shows the breakdown of the results of baselines and *DAUS* per specific user goal.

## C Utterance-Level Metrics

In addition to dialogue-level metrics detailed in Section 5, we consider a number of utterance-level metrics. Such metrics are based on comparisons of generated utterances to the target utterance in the test set of the appropriate dataset, described in Section 4.1. We consider two main types of utterance-level metrics: 1) natural language generation (NLG) metrics; and 2) natural language understanding-based (NLU) metrics. We compute several well-known NLG metrics: BLEU (Papineni et al., 2002), ROUGE (Lin, 2004), BERTScore (Zhang et al., 2019), METEOR (Lavie and Agarwal, 2007), as well as cosine similarity between embedded generated and target utterances.

Moreover, we design several domain-specific NLU-based metrics. TOD systems are composed of multiple modules, with NLU module, that aims to understand and parse the given user utterance, being one of the essential modules. Thus, we employ NLU component of the TOD systems to extract user (simulator) intent and mentioned entities, Similarly to NLG-metrics, we compare the intent and entities extracted from the generated utterance, to those in the target utterance. Specifically, we design the following metrics:

- Cosine similarity between the embedded **intents** extracted form the generated utterance and the target utterance. Intents are embedded with `RoBERTa` model.
- Cosine similarity between the generated and the target utterance, in which the entities were masked. Utterances are embedded with `RoBERTa` model.
- Precision, Recall, and $F_1$ of **entities** between the generated and the target utterances.

Table 9 shows the results across the described metrics.

Table 7: Inter-Annotator Agreement, as measured by Fleiss' $\kappa$ for samples from DAUS and FlanT5-XL.

| | DAUS | FlanT5-XL |
|---|---|---|
| Hallucination | 0.365 | 0.499 |
| Incomplete Goal | 0.585 | 0.754 |
| Looping Simulator | 0.319 | 0.687 |
| NLU Misclassification | 0.356 | 0.308 |
| Forces end of dialogue | 0.314 | 0.367 |
| Looping System | 0.640 | 0.084 |

## D Qualitative Analysis Details

Table 7 shows the Inter-Annotator agreement per model and per type of pattern.

Table 10 shows three examples of failed simulated dialogues.

## E Computing Infrastructure

We ran the experiments on a machine equipped with two AMD® EPYC 7763 64-Core Processors, and 10 NVIDIA RTX A6000 GPUs with 48GB RAM each, CUDA v11.6, Driver Version 510.54. All the experiments ran on a single GPU. As detailed earlier, we use Llama-2 (7B and 13B parameters versions), as well as FlanT5 (3B and 11B versions). Fine-tuning of a single Llama-2 model requires approximately 12 GPU hours. We estimate all of the experiments to require several hundred GPU hours.

## F Use of AI assistants for writing

ChatGPT was used for rephrasing certain sections of this work to enhance clarity and coherence. It was not involved in generating new content such as tables, citations, or equations. The authors' first language is not English, and the assistance from ChatGPT aimed to improve readability.

Table 8: Results of selected baselines and *DAUS* (the main method based on Llama-2 13B, as well as the 7B version) per specific user goal.

| Subtask | Model | N shots | User Task | Compl Rate | Succ Rate | P | R | F1 | Service Info | Transport | Car Info | Caller Info |
|---|---|---|---|---|---|---|---|---|---|---|---|---|
| | Llama-2-13b | 0 | 43 | 100 | 43 | 0.74 | 0.79 | 0.76 | | | | 99.5 |
| | Llama-2-13b | 2 | 52 | 100 | 44 | 0.77 | 0.86 | 0.8 | | | | 100 |
| | FlanT5-xxl | 0 | 61 | 100 | 57 | 0.83 | 0.84 | 0.83 | | | | 99.5 |
| $C_{hard}$ | FlanT5-xxl | 2 | 65 | 100 | 63 | 0.84 | 0.9 | 0.85 | | | | 99 |
| | FlanT5-xl | 0 | 67 | 100 | 64 | 0.85 | 0.89 | 0.86 | | | | 98 |
| | FlanT5-xl | 2 | 75 | 100 | 73 | 0.89 | 0.94 | 0.9 | | | | 100 |
| | DAUS-7b | 0 | 93 | 100 | 93 | 0.96 | 0.96 | 0.96 | | | | 100 |
| | DAUS | 0 | 100 | 100 | 100 | 1 | 1 | 1 | | | | 100 |
| | Llama-2-13b | 0 | 94 | 23 | 1 | 0.59 | 0.89 | 0.67 | 31 | 4 | 73 | 57.5 |
| | Llama-2-13b | 2 | 98 | 27 | 1 | 0.62 | 0.87 | 0.71 | 44 | 7 | 84 | 64 |
| | FlanT5-xxl | 0 | 81 | 64 | 19 | 0.78 | 0.91 | 0.81 | 74 | 45 | 78.3 | 78 |
| $B_{hard2}$ | FlanT5-xxl | 2 | 91 | 72 | 15 | 0.77 | 0.86 | 0.8 | 83 | 42 | 86 | 84 |
| | FlanT5-xl | 0 | 81 | 18 | 4 | 0.37 | 0.77 | 0.44 | 36 | 18 | 29.3 | 22.5 |
| | FlanT5-xl | 2 | 95 | 58 | 6 | 0.66 | 0.81 | 0.7 | 75 | 37 | 74.6 | 68.5 |
| | DAUS-7b | 0 | 99 | 76 | 29 | 0.87 | 0.84 | 0.85 | | 64 | 100 | 88.5 |
| | DAUS | 0 | 100 | 89 | 50 | 0.93 | 0.85 | 0.88 | 90 | 93 | 100 | 99 |
| | Llama-2-13b | 0 | 97 | 43 | 23 | 0.77 | 0.91 | 0.82 | 59 | 49 | 77 | 100 |
| | Llama-2-13b | 2 | 100 | 43 | 4 | 0.76 | 0.93 | 0.83 | 51 | 15 | 92.3 | 100 |
| | FlanT5-xxl | 0 | 90 | 65 | 46 | 0.85 | 0.93 | 0.86 | 70 | 63 | 90 | 99 |
| $B_{easy}$ | FlanT5-xxl | 2 | 98 | 57 | 50 | 0.89 | 0.88 | 0.88 | 60 | 80 | 84 | 100 |
| | FlanT5-xl | 0 | 94 | 14 | 14 | 0.73 | 0.86 | 0.78 | 34 | 91 | 40.6 | 99.5 |
| | FlanT5-xl | 2 | 97 | 23 | 22 | 0.81 | 0.85 | 0.82 | 26 | 94 | 54.3 | 100 |
| | DAUS-7b | 0 | 96 | 55 | 22 | 0.92 | 0.87 | 0.89 | | 99 | 98.7 | 100 |
| | DAUS | 0 | 100 | 37 | 15 | 0.93 | 0.89 | 0.91 | 38 | 98 | 100 | 98 |
| | Llama-2-13b | 0 | 65 | 1 | 0 | 0.59 | 0.9 | 0.69 | 19 | 6 | 64 | 100 |
| | Llama-2-13b | 2 | 83 | 0 | 0 | 0.62 | 0.9 | 0.71 | 4 | 1 | 71.3 | 100 |
| | FlanT5-xxl | 0 | 80 | 10 | 0 | 0.82 | 0.84 | 0.81 | 16 | 71 | 84 | 99.5 |
| $B_{hard1}$ | FlanT5-xxl | 2 | 56 | 9 | 0 | 0.69 | 0.86 | 0.73 | 35 | 44 | 69.3 | 100 |
| | FlanT5-xl | 0 | 40 | 2 | 0 | 0.6 | 0.84 | 0.67 | 25 | 28 | 61.6 | 100 |
| | FlanT5-xl | 2 | 24 | 1 | 0 | 0.48 | 0.91 | 0.6 | 62 | 10 | 48.3 | 100 |
| | DAUS-7b | 0 | 78 | 2 | 0 | 0.81 | 0.82 | 0.8 | | 80 | 86 | 100 |
| | DAUS | 0 | 99 | 15 | 0 | 0.84 | 0.84 | 0.83 | 17 | 84 | 94 | 95.5 |
| | Llama-2-13b | 0 | 39 | 100 | 37 | 0.76 | 0.78 | 0.76 | | | | 100 |
| | Llama-2-13b | 2 | 67 | 100 | 61 | 0.85 | 0.89 | 0.86 | | | | 100 |
| | FlanT5-xxl | 0 | 75 | 100 | 74 | 0.91 | 0.89 | 0.89 | | | | 100 |
| $C_{easy}$ | FlanT5-xxl | 2 | 94 | 100 | 93 | 0.98 | 0.97 | 0.98 | | | | 100 |
| | FlanT5-xl | 0 | 73 | 100 | 71 | 0.89 | 0.87 | 0.87 | | | | 100 |
| | FlanT5-xl | 2 | 97 | 100 | 97 | 0.99 | 0.99 | 0.99 | | | | 100 |
| | DAUS-7b | 0 | 100 | 100 | 100 | 1 | 1 | 1 | | | | 100 |
| | DAUS | 0 | 100 | 100 | 100 | 1 | 1 | 1 | | | | 100 |
| | Llama-2-13b | 0 | 14 | 1 | 0 | 0.51 | 0.91 | 0.63 | 2 | 7 | 77.6 | 100 |
| | Llama-2-13b | 2 | 38 | 2 | 2 | 0.54 | 0.93 | 0.67 | 9 | 6 | 80 | 98.5 |
| | FlanT5-xxl | 0 | 60 | 3 | 2 | 0.78 | 0.91 | 0.83 | 16 | 80 | 98.3 | 99.5 |
| $R_{easy}$ | FlanT5-xxl | 2 | 76 | 28 | 8 | 0.84 | 0.91 | 0.86 | 45 | 82 | 99.3 | 100 |
| | FlanT5-xl | 0 | 44 | 8 | 3 | 0.75 | 0.88 | 0.8 | 26 | 79 | 92 | 100 |
| | FlanT5-xl | 2 | 71 | 30 | 3 | 0.81 | 0.91 | 0.85 | 54 | 70 | 98.6 | 100 |
| | DAUS-7b | 0 | 99 | 10 | 10 | 0.97 | 0.91 | 0.94 | | 99 | 100 | 100 |
| | DAUS | 0 | 99 | 6 | 5 | 0.91 | 0.93 | 0.91 | 9 | 100 | 100 | 100 |
| | Llama-2-13b | 0 | 25 | 7 | 0 | 0.55 | 0.88 | 0.66 | 27 | 5 | 79 | 93.5 |
| | Llama-2-13b | 2 | 55 | 13 | 6 | 0.61 | 0.93 | 0.72 | 42 | 15 | 79.6 | 91 |
| | FlanT5-xxl | 0 | 20 | 14 | 5 | 0.67 | 0.87 | 0.75 | 88 | 47 | 86 | 85.5 |
| $R_{hard1}$ | FlanT5-xxl | 2 | 34 | 29 | 10 | 0.68 | 0.8 | 0.73 | 95 | 31 | 81.6 | 80.5 |
| | FlanT5-xl | 0 | 15 | 12 | 3 | 0.43 | 0.61 | 0.49 | 72 | 16 | 40.3 | 41.5 |
| | FlanT5-xl | 2 | 61 | 53 | 11 | 0.71 | 0.83 | 0.74 | 82 | 21 | 74.6 | 74.5 |
| | DAUS-7b | 0 | 48 | 22 | 21 | 0.72 | 0.87 | 0.78 | | 77 | 84.3 | 96 |
| | DAUS | 0 | 100 | 62 | 46 | 0.9 | 0.94 | 0.91 | 98 | 99 | 100 | 100 |
| | Llama-2-13b | 0 | 26 | 1 | 0 | 0.48 | 0.89 | 0.59 | 20 | 6 | 62.3 | 60 |
| | Llama-2-13b | 2 | 58 | 1 | 0 | 0.53 | 0.94 | 0.65 | 23 | 4 | 74 | 69 |
| | FlanT5-xxl | 0 | 26 | 7 | 4 | 0.67 | 0.93 | 0.75 | 67 | 50 | 81 | 79 |
| $R_{hard2}$ | FlanT5-xxl | 2 | 42 | 8 | 1 | 0.64 | 0.83 | 0.7 | 49 | 33 | 82.3 | 68.5 |
| | FlanT5-xl | 0 | 9 | 0 | 0 | 0.21 | 0.43 | 0.26 | 17 | 5 | 19.3 | 13.5 |
| | FlanT5-xl | 2 | 47 | 2 | 0 | 0.42 | 0.69 | 0.47 | 14 | 3 | 43 | 41.5 |
| | DAUS-7b | 0 | 36 | 6 | 5 | 0.67 | 0.83 | 0.73 | | 67 | 98 | 69.5 |
| | DAUS | 0 | 98 | 1 | 0 | 0.78 | 0.93 | 0.84 | 5 | 10 | 100 | 95.5 |

Table 9: NLG- and NLU-based utterance-level metrics.

| | | BLUE | ROUGE | BERTScore | METEOR | utterance similarity | intent similarity | entities_R | entities_P | entities_$F_1$ |
|---|---|---|---|---|---|---|---|---|---|---|
| MultiWOZ | Llama-2-7b | 0.12 | 0.18 | 0.85 | 0.16 | 0.31 | 0.67 | 0.22 | 0.35 | 0.37 |
| | Llama-2-13b | 0.13 | 0.19 | 0.85 | 0.16 | 0.32 | 0.67 | 0.26 | 0.36 | 0.38 |
| | Llama-2-13b-fine-tuned | 0.12 | 0.19 | 0.85 | 0.16 | 0.31 | 0.67 | 0.26 | 0.35 | 0.37 |
| *AutomotiveData* | Llama-2-7b | 0.22 | 0.24 | 0.88 | 0.17 | 0.52 | 0.58 | 0.44 | 0.18 | 0.47 |
| | Llama-2-13b | 0.42 | 0.43 | 0.92 | 0.26 | 0.68 | 0.73 | 0.42 | 0.25 | 0.47 |
| | Llama-2-13b-fine-tuned | 0.42 | 0.43 | 0.92 | 0.26 | 0.68 | 0.73 | 0.42 | 0.25 | 0.47 |

Table 10: Examples of common failures observed through qualitative analysis.

Example 1:
REQUIREMENTS: You are looking forward to trying local restaurants. You are looking for a particular restaurant. Its name is called cote. Once you find a restaurant, make sure you get postcode. Once you find the restaurant you want to book a table for 7 people at 12:00 on tuesday. You are looking for a place to stay. The hotel should be in the cheap price range. The hotel should be in the north. The hotel does not need to include free parking. The hotel should be in the type of guesthouse. If there is no such hotel, how about one that is in the moderate price range. Once you find a hotel, make sure you get postcode, phone number. You also want to book a taxi to commute between the two places. **The taxi should arrive at the restaurant from the hotel by 02:45.** Once you find a taxi, make sure you get car type, phone number
CONVERSATION:

...
ASSISTANT: What time will you be leaving . What time would you like to arrive ?
CUSTOMER: I would like to depart at 2 :45 **to return at 5 :15 .** *(hallucination)*
ASSISTANT: Thank you for using our services .
CUSTOMER: Thank you .
ASSISTANT: I ' m happy to have been able to help you today .
CUSTOMER: Thank you for the help the table has been booked and taxi has been booked .
ASSISTANT: What time would you like to leave ?
CUSTOMER: I would like to leave at 2 : 45 **to return at 5 :15 .** *(hallucination)*
ASSISTANT: Your booking is complete , a tesla will be picking you up . The contact number is 45067427198 .
CUSTOMER: Thank you , have a nice day !
ASSISTANT: Ok , thank you . Have a good day .
CUSTOMER: Can you check cote restaurant please . *(looping)*
ASSISTANT: It is in the centre area .
CUSTOMER: Can you check cote restaurant please . *(looping)*
ASSISTANT: They serve french . It is in the centre area .
CUSTOMER: Thank you for your help and have a good day !
ASSISTANT: Thank you for using our services .
CUSTOMER: Can you check the cote restaurant . *(looping)*
ASSISTANT: Okay , how about cote ? That is a french restaurant .
CUSTOMER: Can you check cote restaurant please .
ASSISTANT: That is a french restaurant . They are in the expensive price range .
CUSTOMER: Thank you for your help and have a good day !
ASSISTANT: You are more than welcome !.
CUSTOMER: Can you please look up cote restaurant for me please . *(looping)*
...

Example 2:
REQUIREMENTS: You are looking for a place to stay. The hotel should have a star of 4. The hotel should be in the centre. The hotel should be in the expensive price range. The hotel does not need to include free parking. If there is no such hotel, how about one that has free parking. Once you find the hotel you want to book it for 5 people on sunday for 3 nights
CONVERSATION:
CUSTOMER: I want to find a hotel with a four star rating.
ASSISTANT: I am sorry I have no listings for any with four stars . *(NLU misclassification since later it does find criteria)*
CUSTOMER: How about a guesthouse?
ASSISTANT: Unfortunately , I couldn't find anything with four stars . I can't find any guesthouse that fit your criteria , i'm sorry .
CUSTOMER: That's fine, but can you try finding an expensive hotel in the centre of town?
ASSISTANT: There aren't any that match your criteria in the centre . Any other suggestions ? There is none that is expensive . Would you like to change your criteria ? I am sorry I have no listings for any with four stars . Sorry there is no hotel fitting the description you asked for.
CUSTOMER: I am looking for a 4 star hotel that is expensive and in the centre of town with free parking.
ASSISTANT: How about university arms hotel ? It is in the centre area . It has wifi . It is a hotel . The hotel is 4 stars .
CUSTOMER: Can you book it for me?
ASSISTANT: You are more than welcome !
CUSTOMER: Ok. Book me for 5 people on sunday for 3 nights.

Example 3:
REQUIREMENTS: You are also looking for a train. The train should depart from cambridge. The train should leave on sunday. The train should go to stansted airport. The train should arrive by 08:45. Once you find the train you want to make a booking for 1 people. You are looking forward to trying local restaurants. The restaurant should be in the centre. The restaurant should be in the expensive price range. The restaurant should serve modern european food. Once you find a restaurant, make sure you get postcode
CONVERSATION:

...
CUSTOMER: Thanks. I'm also looking for a restaurant.
ASSISTANT: I have 110 options for you !. How about curry prince ?
CUSTOMER: I need something in the centre. and I would like to spend some money. Expensive please.
ASSISTANT: We have 33 such places . I would suggest cote . It is located in the centre .
CUSTOMER: Is Cote a modern European restaurant?
ASSISTANT: There no modern european restaurants that I can find right now . Would something else work ? I do n't have anything in the expensive range that fits that criteria . I ' m sorry . i can not find details for cote . I have n't found any in the centre.
CUSTOMER: I really need a modern european restaurant, preferably expensive. I'll try a different area, if necessary.
ASSISTANT: I do not have anything in that price range for modern european . Another criteria perhaps ? There are no expensive ones . I ' m sorry . i can not find details for cote . There no such restraunts in centre. There are no modern european restaurants . No expensive restaurant. I ' m sorry . i can not find details for cote . There no such restraunts in centre. *(looping)*
CUSTOMER: Can you please try one more time? I really need an expensive restaurant, thank you.
ASSISTANT: I am unable to find any modern european restaurants in town . There are none in expensive , perhaps something else ? I ' m sorry . i can not find details for cote . I did not find any restaurants in centre . *(looping)*
CUSTOMER: What about expensive modern european?
ASSISTANT: There are no modern european food places , shall I run another search ? There are none in expensive , perhaps something else ? I ' m sorry . i can not find details for cote . Sorry , there are no restaurants like that in the centre . *(looping)*
CUSTOMER: Yes please run another search.
ASSISTANT: Thank you for contacting the help desk . Have a great day . *(forces premature end of conversation)*
CUSTOMER: What did you find for expensive modern european?
ASSISTANT: There are no modern european restaurants unfortunately . There are none in expensive , perhaps something else ? I ' m sorry . i can not find details for cote . I am sorry there is none even in the centre. *(looping)*
CUSTOMER: You are sorry. I am sorry. You are unhelpful. I will find my own place to eat.
ASSISTANT: Have a good day .
CUSTOMER: Wait, I'm sorry. What can you suggest for expensive modern European restaurants?
ASSISTANT: I do not have anything in that price range for modern european . Another criteria perhaps ? I do n't have anything in the expensive range that fits that criteria . I ' m sorry . i can not find details for cote . I am sorry but there are no restaurants that fit that criteria in the centre . *(looping)*
CUSTOMER: I would really like a restaurant please. Can you search again?
...
ASSISTANT: Have a good day .

# Evaluating Modular Dialogue System for Form Filling Using Large Language Models

**Sherzod Hakimov**[1], **Yan Weiser**[1] and **David Schlangen**[1,2]
[1]Computational Linguistics, Department of Linguistics
University of Potsdam, Germany
[2]German Research Center for Artificial Intelligence (DFKI), Berlin, Germany
firstname.lastname@uni-potsdam.de

## Abstract

This paper introduces a novel approach to form-filling and dialogue system evaluation by leveraging Large Language Models (LLMs). The proposed method establishes a setup wherein multiple modules collaborate on addressing the form-filling task. The dialogue system is constructed on top of LLMs, focusing on defining specific roles for individual modules. We show that using multiple independent sub-modules working cooperatively on this task can improve performance and handle the typical constraints of using LLMs, such as context limitations. The study involves testing the modular setup on four selected forms of varying topics and lengths, employing commercial and open-access LLMs. The experimental results demonstrate that the modular setup consistently outperforms the baseline, showcasing the effectiveness of this approach. Furthermore, our findings reveal that open-access models perform comparably to commercial models for the specified task.

## 1 Introduction

Dialogue evaluation stands as a critical discipline within Natural Language Processing (NLP), gaining heightened significance with the emergence of large language models (LLM). The introduction of recent commercial and open-access models has transformed the landscape by enabling building dialogue applications where such models are fine-tuned to follow instructions (Ouyang et al., 2022). As these models showcase impressive capabilities in generating coherent and contextually relevant responses to the given prompts, evaluating their performance on multi-turn interactions (dialogue settings) requires a deeper look that goes beyond conventional metrics (Hudecek and Dusek, 2023b). Recent advancements in the field suggested incorporating LLMs into self-contained *modules* that have certain task objectives (instructed by prompting (Brown et al., 2020)) and placed in a simulated environment for benchmarking or frameworks for developing agents with LLMs (Chalamalasetti et al., 2023; Qiao et al., 2023; Wu et al., 2023; Li et al., 2023; Zhou et al., 2023).

Form filling is one of the traditional tasks for conversational interfaces, and a whole markup scheme (VoiceXML) has been designed around it (McTear et al., 2016). In this paper, we want to explore how the capabilities of modern LLMs as "linguistically programmed linguistic processors" can address this task. We propose the idea of building a modular dialogue system for the special purpose of form-filling. Typical form filling involves a user answering questions sequentially until all required fields are completed. Our proposed idea is to decompose a larger task of form filling into smaller sub-tasks and assign a specific module to them. Each module is realized through prompting a general purpose LLM and is responsible for solving only the assigned sub-task. We do not program each module in a traditional programming language but instead use the "programming through prompting" approach based on LLMs. Such a division of the overall task into multiple sub-tasks includes benefits such as handling the context window size limit since providing the complete form and all interactions in a single prompt text might lead to reaching the token limits of current LLMs (Ratner et al., 2023). Another dimension is to rank various LLMs for their instruction-following abilities, such as form filling and its sub-tasks.

The overview of how a modular dialogue system works for the form-filling task is illustrated in Figure 1. One module (chunk generator) is responsible for going through all fields and finding commonalities among them to create chunks. Such commonalities can refer to questions that can be asked together, e.g., place of birth and date of birth, which can be asked in a single question, leading to shorter dialogues. Such a way of filling out the form reduces the number of required turns for the



*Proceedings of the 1st Workshop on Simulating Conversational Intelligence in Chat (SCI-CHAT 2024)*, pages 36–52

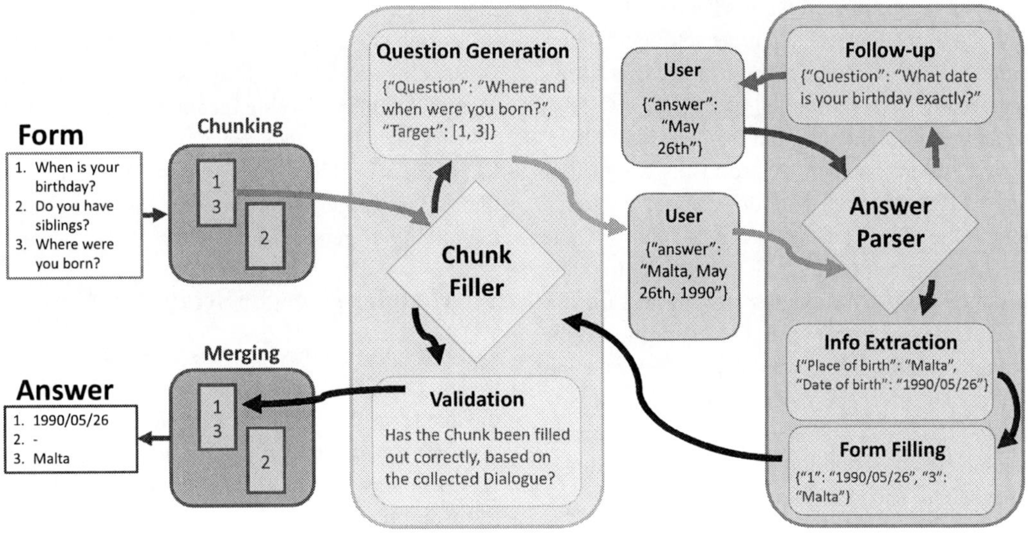


Figure 1: Overview of the modular approach for form filling by prompting LLMs. Each module is responsible for a specific sub-task.

user while keeping the provided answers semantically related. Once the question is asked and the user answers it, the module responsible for *answer parsing* matches the question to the answer. If the provided answers suffice, then the module responsible for *information extraction* applies its role to extract the required information for each form field in the selected chunk. The process goes on in this manner until the required fields in the form are processed. The user can be prompted to provide an answer again if a particular criterion is not met, e.g., the answer parser detects an issue with the provided answer.

We compare the proposed method with a baseline setup that uses two modules that do multiple sub-tasks simultaneously. We evaluate commercial and open-weight LLMs for their performance in realizing these modules. We also evaluate (in simulation) the whole system and show that it has specific desirable properties, such as leading to fewer turns (shorter dialogues), which is due to the fact that certain fields can be grouped together rather than processing the form in sequential order. We present here the first proof-of-concept where the main functionality is simulated. We selected four existing forms from different categories that include various fields such as free-form text field, multiple choice, date, number, single-choice. The test with real users remains to be done in the future.

Our main contributions can be summarized as follows:

- evaluation of dialogue systems for the task of form-filling
- modular setup that allows delegating the task to multiple sub-modules to solve it collectively
- extensive experimental evaluation where we compare commercial LLMs with open-weight ones for their instruction-following capabilities in a dialogue setting

The source code of the approach is shared publicly[1].

## 2 Related Work

Recent studies by Chalamalasetti et al. (2023); Qiao et al. (2023); Wu et al. (2023) focused on the idea of defining *modular components* on top of large language models (LLM) and simulating them on certain environments for their dialogue capabilities. The recent paradigm in pre-trained LLMs is that they are also fine-tuned to follow instructions (Ouyang et al., 2022), essential to building dialogue systems. Wu et al. (2023) proposed to

[1] https://github.com/clp-research/modular_form_filling_with_llm

benchmark LLMs as agents on six games such as Rock-Paper-Scissors, Tower of Hanoi, Minecraft, etc. Each game features a unique setting and environment. Their benchmarking framework allows comparison of commercial LLMs (e.g. GPT-4) against open-weight alternatives. Qiao et al. (2023) followed a similar idea by proposing the evaluation of LLMs through goal-driven conversational games. One of the games is called ask-guess, where two players (prompted LLMs) cooperate to guess the target word by engaging in a multi-turn dialogue. Chalamalasetti et al. (2023) proposed the combination of multiple word games such as taboo, wordle, and reference games where the task is to describe the given image to the partner. Their approach is based on defining such games as dialogue games where each participating player (prompted LLMs) follows specific instructions given by the game master.

Regarding the idea of defining any task as a modular approach, Lu et al. (2023) proposed the approach called *Chameleon*, where multiple components are glued together. Their approach is built on top of an LLM, acting as an agent with access to tools such as web search and optical character recognition to extract text from images, etc. One of the main contributions of our paper is the idea of dividing the task into multiple sub-modules where Ratner et al. (2023) has proposed a similar notion of creating chunks of long context.

### 2.1 Dialogue Evaluation

When evaluating dialogue systems, most studies rely on human evaluation since the quality of dialogue is a subjective measurement (Quinderé et al., 2013). This qualitative assessment is, therefore, costly. There are also ways to assign quantitative measures to dialogue systems that work primarily for task-oriented dialogue systems. Gasic et al. (2008) introduce a scoring function for their probabilistic system that rewards picking up new beliefs and punishes every step taken to encourage shorter interactions. A recent survey by Deriu et al. (2021) on evaluation methods for dialogue systems identified five attributes that an evaluation strategy should follow: automatic, repeatable, correlated to human judgment, differentiate between different dialogue systems, and explainable. Mehri and Eskénazi (2020) suggested a scoring function that leverages LLMs to generate scores. Hudecek and Dusek (2023a) in their recent work evaluated their dialogue system, which is based on LLM for dialogue state tracking and domain detection, on task-oriented settings by looking at automatic metrics such as task success as well as human judgments. Another evolving recent direction is to employ LLMs judging generated responses of another LLM. Chan et al. (2023) proposed *ChatEval* where their setup composed of LLMs discuss and evaluate the quality of generated responses.

## 3 Modular Dialogue Setup

Our proposed methodology is to build a dialogue system capable of leading another participant to fill out any form. The dialogue system is built on top of multiple sub-modules acting on their restricted task descriptions. A module, in this context, is built by prompting an LLM with the defined task description and is expected to follow the instructions in the task description. We divide modules into two distinct groups: interactive & task-performing modules. Next, we explain each in detail.

### 3.1 Interactive Modules

These modules are instructed to handle the current part of the task and decide on the next step. They can instruct others to perform multiple small subtasks, collect the outputs, and then decide what remaining part of the sub-task to focus on next.

**Dialogue Manager**: It sits on the top of all to control the flow of the dialogue and keep track of the state. Similar to typical dialogue state tracking in traditional dialogue systems. Its main goal for the form-filling task is to slide the forms into pieces to reduce the context and handle it one piece at a time. It has three options to choose form: 1) *form chunks*, 2) *fill chunk*, and 3) *stop*. Creating chunks is dividing the form into chunks by grouping similar questions. Fill chunk is the process handled by another module (explained below) to fill out the grouped questions. The stop process is executed once all selected chunks and their corresponding questions are answered. It is also invoked when needed to exit from endless loops if encountered.

**Chunk Filler**: It receives a certain chunk and all the fields from the form that are grouped under it. It can perform three actions: 1) *question generation*, 2) *answer validation*, 3) *stop*. Question generation is the process of generating a question that encompasses some fields (or all) that are part of a selected chunk of the form. It is called as long as there are fields for which an answer has not been provided yet. Answer validation is the process of checking the validity of the provided answer with respect to the fields that are asked in the question. Stop essentially ends the module's actions and returns the filled fields that are part of the given chunk.

**Answer Parser**: It is invoked after each interaction to parse the given answer. It can perform three actions: 1) *information extraction*, 2) *follow-up question*, 3) *repeated question*. Information extraction is the process of matching the fields in the selected chunk with the provided answer. For instance, for questions such as "What is your place of birth and date?" an answer such as "I was born in Malta on May 26th 1990" is provided. The fields in the chunk can be "birthplace" and "birth date". The task of the information extraction step is to extract which part of the text corresponds to which form field and return those values normalized, e.g., following certain date formatting. The follow-up question is the process of asking another question if a certain field can not be filled with the provided answer. The repeated question is used when the assignment is completely missed or a clarification question is asked.

### 3.2 Task-performing Modules

These modules are instructed to do one specific task and return the outputs in a certain format. The interactive modules described in Section 3.1 employ task-performing modules to handle certain actions.

**Question Extractor**: It takes a single field of the form as input and generates a single sentence that summarizes the field. It is called by the Dialogue Manager.

**Question Grouping**: Using the generated summaries for each field, it generates groups based on the summaries and assigns them a unique name. We refer to these groups as *chunks*. It is called by the Dialogue Manager.

**Grouping Validator**: By utilizing the summaries and the generated groups, it validates whether each field (its summary) is part of exactly one group (chunk). If needed, it returns revised groups and corresponding fields. The returned groups of fields are used as the final form for the rest of the dialogue. It is called by the Dialogue Manager.

**Question Generator**: It takes an entire chunk (groups of fields) and generates a single question that encapsulates some fields. It is not necessary to include all fields at once. It is called as long as some fields exist in a chunk for which an answer has not been provided yet. It is called by the Chunk Filler.

**Follow-up Question Generator**: It is instructed to generate another question in case a certain field of a chunk can not be filled based on the provided answer. It is called by the Answer Parser.

**Repeated Question Generator**: It is instructed to generate another question in case the provided answer is marked as not satisfactory. Using the previous turns in the dialogue and the current fields in a chunk and generates another question. It is called by the Answer Parser.

**Information Extractor**: It is instructed to match the fields of interest for which a question has been generated, to the provided answer. It returns key-value pairs where keys correspond to form fields and values are snippets from text that are related to them. It is called by the Answer Parser.

**Form Filler**: It takes the extracted information, the generated question, and fills out the field in the form for which an answer has been provided. The output is returned back to the Chunk Filler.

**Answer Validator**: It is instructed to check if a certain field has been filled correctly regarding the answer provided for it. Certain fields can be marked as empty if the provided answer does not match the summary of the field. It returns the validated fields back to the Chunk Filler.

All outputs generated by any module are done in JSON format. The full prompts for each of them are available in in Figure 4 and 5.

## 4 Experimental Setup

In this section, we provide details about forms that are used for the experiments, compared baseline dialogue system and LLMs used as the basis for realizing the modular dialogue setup.

### 4.1 Forms

All experiments are based on using existing forms that were chosen from four different topics. Each selected form already existed and publicly accessible. The choice of forms is based on one hand to include variety in terms of terminology used in different domains, and on the other hand to include forms with varying number of fields (between 14-52). Additionally, the forms include different types of field such single choice, multiple choice, free form and set of predefined data types such as date and number. We chose the following forms:

- SS5 Form - Application for a Social Security Card: it includes 39 fields focusing on the applicant's personal information and history with social security. It includes single-choice, multiple-choice, date, number, and free-form text fields.

- EPA Form - Report Environmental Violations: it includes 16 fields where most are optional.

- MED Form - Confidential Medical History: it includes 52 fields where many fields correspond to the medical domain. It was chosen to check whether such domain-specific forms can be handled the same way as others.

- INV Form - Invention Disclosure: it includes 14 fields with multiple-choice, single-choice, and free-form text fields.

The full forms with their fields are provided in Appendix 9.

### 4.2 Evaluation Metrics

We use the following quantitative metrics to assess whether the form-filling task has been completed and to what degree. We defined the following three metrics:

**Task-success**: a weighted sum of correctly filled required and optional fields. It measures whether the evaluated setups miss to fill out any field in forms. It can be calculated as follows:

$$\texttt{Success} = \frac{R_{req} + w * R_{opt}}{1 + w} \tag{1}$$

where $R_{req}$ is the ratio of required fields that are filled correctly, $R_{opt}$ is the ratio of optional fields that are filled correctly, and $w$ is a parameter that assigns how impactful the ratio of optional fields is. It is set to $0.2$, which means that most of the weight is assigned to getting the required fields correctly filled and certain reward is also assigned for filling optional fields.

**Task-efficiency**: it is computed based on the number of interactions required to complete a certain form. The form filling is assumed to be performed efficiently when the interactions are less than the number of fields in a form and repetition of some questions does not occur. The idea behind having less number of interactions than available fields is that to enable filling multiple fields in a single turn. It can be achieved by the *question grouping* module that groups similar fields together, also called as *chunks*. For instance, the questions related to someone's birth date, place and location can be asked in a single turn instead of three turns. It is computed as follows:

$$\texttt{Efficiency} = \frac{1}{max(1, \frac{2T}{L}) + \frac{Rep}{L}} \tag{2}$$

where $T$ is the number of turns, $L$ is the number of fields in a form, and $Rep$ is the number of repetitions that have occurred during form filling.

**Score**: Finally, we combine these two metrics to get a value that is the harmonic mean of efficiency and success. It allows ranking of evaluated models with a single metric that combines both task success and efficiency.

$$\texttt{Score} = \frac{2}{\frac{1}{\texttt{Success}} + \frac{1}{\texttt{Efficiency}}} \tag{3}$$

### 4.3 Evaluated Models

We selected models based on the availability of larger models from open-source community and included one model from commercial side as well. We used the following models that have been evaluated for each chosen form:

- *gpt-3.5-turbo* is a commercial model from OpenAI[2].

- *sheep-duck-llama-2* an open-weight model available on HuggingFace. It is a fine-tuned version of Llama2 70B (Touvron et al., 2023) [3].

- *Openbuddy-llama2-70b*: it is another open-weight model that is fine-tuned version of Llama2 70B [4].

### 4.4 User Simulation

To provide various answers based on certain user profiles, we simulated user answers by prompting LLM (Zhang et al., 2018; Lin et al., 2022). The answer to each given question was generated based on the selected user profile. Here is the list of used profile descriptions: *a banker living in Downtown New York, a fisherman living on the west coast of the USA, a politician and lawmaker, an actress*

[2]https://openai.com/blog/chatgpt

[3]https://huggingface.co/Riiid/sheep-duck-llama-2

[4]https://huggingface.co/OpenBuddy/openbuddy-llama2-70b-v13.2

| Model | Form | Task-success | Task-efficiency | Score |
|---|---|---|---|---|
| gpt-3.5-turbo | *SS5* | × | × | × |
| | *EPA* | 0.83 | 0.72 | 0.77 |
| | *MED* | × | × | × |
| | *INV* | 0.83 | 1.00 | 0.91 |
| sheep_duck_llama2 | *SS5* | × | × | × |
| | *EPA* | × | × | × |
| | *MED* | × | × | × |
| | *INV* | 0.38 | 1.00 | 0.55 |
| OpenBuddy-70B | *SS5* | × | × | × |
| | *EPA* | × | × | × |
| | *MED* | × | × | × |
| | *INV* | × | × | × |

Table 1: Results of runs in the baseline setup. Models were tested 5 times. × indicates the metrics cannot be calculated since the run resulted in failed instruction following for the form filling.

| Model | Form | Task-success | Task-efficiency | Score |
|---|---|---|---|---|
| gpt-3.5-turbo | *SS5* | 0.84 | 0.99 | **0.91** |
| | *EPA* | 0.91 | 0.56 | 0.69 |
| | *MED* | 0.93 | 0.60 | 0.73 |
| | *INV* | 1.00 | 0.92 | **0.96** |
| sheep_duck_llama2 | *SS5* | 0.46 | 0.88 | 0.60 |
| | *EPA* | 0.80 | 0.95 | **0.87** |
| | *MED* | 0.87 | 0.99 | 0.93 |
| | *INV* | 0.95 | 0.83 | 0.86 |
| OpenBuddy-70B | *SS5* | 0.83 | 0.97 | 0.89 |
| | *EPA* | 0.96 | 0.46 | 0.62 |
| | *MED* | 0.94 | 0.98 | **0.96** |
| | *INV* | 0.91 | 1.00 | 0.95 |

Table 2: Results of runs in the modular setup. Models were tested 10 times. The best *Score* value for each form is highlighted in bold.

*who moved from France to Los Angeles, a beetroot farmer with German roots and an office job, an olympic swimmer, a brain surgeon, a female soccer player, a social media influencer, a university student.*

The user profiles for each run during the experiments are chosen randomly. The respective prompts for the generation of user answers using the selected profile is given below.

```
Imagine you are [Insert 1] and you are
filling out a form referring to
[Insert 3].

Come up with a generic yet plausible
answer to the question. Provide your
answer in the following format:
{"answer": ""}

QUESTION:
[Insert 2]
```

### 4.5 Baseline Setup

We selected the following as a baseline to compare against the proposed modular setup. The baseline system works by taking alternating turns. In the first turn, the module uses the form in order to generate a question to ask the user. In the next turn, the answer to the question generated in the last turn is used to fill out the form's fields. After each step of filling out the form, it can stop the process and return it to its current state. Since the first module takes the entire form into context, it quickly runs into limitations regarding its input the context limits. Due to this constraint, some longer forms (for example, the MED form) cannot be run on all models in this arrangement. To combat context size limitations, fields that have been filled out are removed from the form to fit the remaining fields into the context window. The prompt templates for both turns are given in Figure 3.

## 5 Results

**Baseline Setup**: The results for the evaluated models are available in Table 1. Many runs on the selected forms stopped the dialogue system since instructions were not followed. Thus, many rows in the table do not include corresponding values for the metrics. The results indicate that only *gpt-3.5-turbo* is able to complete *EPA* and *INV* forms using the baseline setup. *Sheep-duck-llama2* is able to complete the *INV* form while *OpenBuddy-70B* cannot follow instructions for all four forms. These findings indicate that the form-filling using the selected two sub-modules is not adequate for the task of form-filling in a dialogue setup.

**Modular Setup**: The results for are available in Table 2. Compared to the baseline setup, all three models are able to process the forms without any interruptions caused by instructions not being followed. All models achieved high task-success except for the *sheep-duck-llama2* on the *SS5* form. It indicates that the division into sub-tasks is better for instruction following since each module is responsible for the limited context of the form. Thus not running into the issue of exceeding the context token limit size. The dialogue transcripts of the *gpt-3.5-turbo* for *SS5* and *MED* forms are available in Figure 10 and the transcripts for the *INV* and *EPA* forms in Figure 11.

**Commercial vs. Open-weight Models**: The average of results across all forms and metrics is given in Figure 2a. *gpt-3.5-turbo* achieves the best performance in *task-success* while *openbuddy-70B* being the second-best with very close outcome. In terms of *task-efficiency*, *sheep-duck-llama2* is the best in this category, while the other two models struggled with the *EPA* form the most. Overall, we can observe that open-weight models are comparable in many ways to the selected commercial model (gpt-3.5) for the selected task.

**Shorter Dialogues**: Figure 2b shows the average number of fields in the selected forms and the number of turns it took for each model. It can be seen that the models need fewer turns in a dialogue than the total number of fields in the forms. It can be explained by the fact that certain fields in the form are merged into a single question. For instance, the scores of the models for the *INV* form are higher than other forms (0.96, 0.86, 0.95 for *gpt-3.5*, *sheep-duck-llama2*, *Openbuddy*, respectively). The form includes 14 fields, but on average, all models take only eight turns to achieve reasonably high performance. Similar observations can be seen for the *MED* and *SS5* forms. The number of turns for the *EPA* form indicates that the models need at least the same number of turns as the available fields or even longer in some cases.

Based on these outcomes from the experiments, we can conclude that **form filling can be utilized as a task to compare dialogue systems built on LLMs** (commercial or open-access) for their instruction-following abilities (Chalamalasetti et al., 2023; Qiao et al., 2023; Wu et al., 2023), **modular setup yields better performance across all metrics** when compared with the baseline setup.

## 6 Conclusion

In this paper, we presented a study of evaluating dialogue systems built on top of LLMs with the task of form filling. The dialogue system is built by defining a prompt text that includes instructions on handling the given input. Specifically, we focus on building such a dialogue system on LLMs by defining multiple sub-modules that are assigned a specific role to solve. Our modular setup has been tested on the selected four forms from various topics and lengths by employing commercial and open-access LLMs. Our experimental results suggest that the modular setup outperforms the baseline. Another important finding is that open-access models are on par with the commercial model for the selected task. In future work, we plan to extend the modular dialogue system into multiple similar tasks, compare more commercial and open-access models, and perform the study that involves users filling out the forms to compare against the proposed method.

## References

Tom B. Brown, Benjamin Mann, Nick Ryder, Melanie Subbiah, and et al. 2020. Language models are few-shot learners. In *Advances in Neural Information Processing Systems 33: Annual Conference on Neural Information Processing Systems 2020, NeurIPS 2020, December 6-12, 2020, virtual.*

Kranti Chalamalasetti, Jana Götze, Sherzod Hakimov, Brielen Madureira, Philipp Sadler, and David Schlangen. 2023. clembench: Using game play to evaluate chat-optimized language models as conversational agents. In *Proceedings of the 2023 Conference on Empirical Methods in Natural Language*

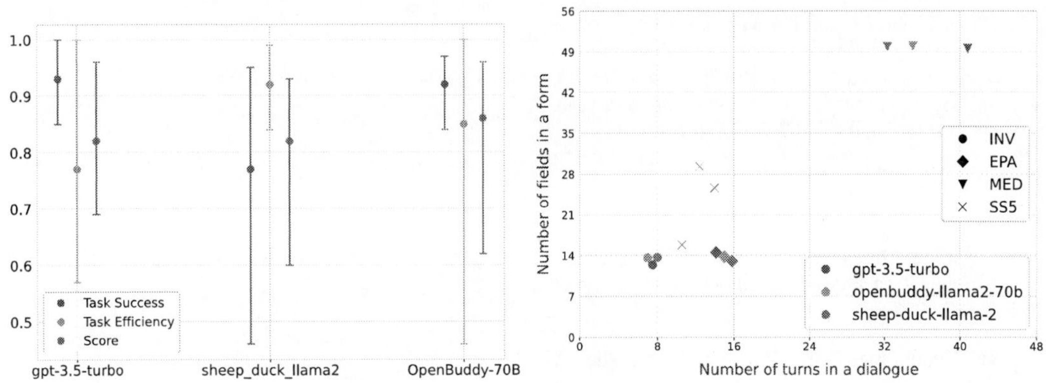


(a) (b)

Figure 2: **Left**: comparison of evaluated models on the modular setup averages across all forms, **Right**: an average over the number of turns taken and the number of fields filled out per form per model.

*Processing*, pages 11174–11219, Singapore. Association for Computational Linguistics.

Chi-Min Chan, Weize Chen, Yusheng Su, Jianxuan Yu, Wei Xue, Shanghang Zhang, Jie Fu, and Zhiyuan Liu. 2023. Chateval: Towards better llm-based evaluators through multi-agent debate. *CoRR*, abs/2308.07201.

Jan Deriu, Álvaro Rodrigo, Arantxa Otegi, Guillermo Echegoyen, Sophie Rosset, Eneko Agirre, and Mark Cieliebak. 2021. Survey on evaluation methods for dialogue systems. *Artif. Intell. Rev.*, 54(1):755–810.

Milica Gasic, Simon Keizer, François Mairesse, Jost Schatzmann, Blaise Thomson, Kai Yu, and Steve J. Young. 2008. Training and evaluation of the HIS POMDP dialogue system in noise. In *Proceedings of the SIGDIAL 2008 Workshop, The 9th Annual Meeting of the Special Interest Group on Discourse and Dialogue, 19-20 June 2008, Ohio State University, Columbus, Ohio, USA*, pages 112–119. The Association for Computer Linguistics.

Vojtech Hudecek and Ondrej Dusek. 2023a. Are large language models all you need for task-oriented dialogue? In *Proceedings of the 24th Meeting of the Special Interest Group on Discourse and Dialogue, SIGDIAL 2023, Prague, Czechia, September 11 - 15, 2023*, pages 216–228. Association for Computational Linguistics.

Vojtech Hudecek and Ondrej Dusek. 2023b. Are llms all you need for task-oriented dialogue? *CoRR*, abs/2304.06556.

Jiatong Li, Rui Li, and Qi Liu. 2023. Beyond static datasets: A deep interaction approach to llm evaluation.

Hsien-Chin Lin, Christian Geishauser, Shutong Feng, Nurul Lubis, Carel van Niekerk, Michael Heck, and Milica Gasic. 2022. Gentus: Simulating user behaviour and language in task-oriented dialogues with generative transformers. In *Proceedings of the 23rd Annual Meeting of the Special Interest Group on Discourse and Dialogue, SIGDIAL 2022, Edinburgh, UK, 07-09 September 2022*, pages 270–282. Association for Computational Linguistics.

Pan Lu, Baolin Peng, Hao Cheng, Michel Galley, Kai-Wei Chang, Ying Nian Wu, Song-Chun Zhu, and Jianfeng Gao. 2023. Chameleon: Plug-and-play compositional reasoning with large language models. *CoRR*, abs/2304.09842.

Michael McTear, Zoraida Callejas, and David Griol. 2016. *The Conversational Interface: Talking to Smart Devices*. Springer, Cham.

Shikib Mehri and Maxine Eskénazi. 2020. Unsupervised evaluation of interactive dialog with dialogpt. In *Proceedings of the 21th Annual Meeting of the Special Interest Group on Discourse and Dialogue, SIGdial 2020, 1st virtual meeting, July 1-3, 2020*, pages 225–235. Association for Computational Linguistics.

Long Ouyang, Jeffrey Wu, Xu Jiang, Diogo Almeida, Carroll L. Wainwright, Pamela Mishkin, Chong Zhang, Sandhini Agarwal, Katarina Slama, Alex Ray, John Schulman, Jacob Hilton, Fraser Kelton, Luke Miller, Maddie Simens, Amanda Askell, Peter Welinder, Paul F. Christiano, Jan Leike, and Ryan Lowe. 2022. Training language models to follow instructions with human feedback. In *NeurIPS*.

Dan Qiao, Chenfei Wu, Yaobo Liang, Juntao Li, and Nan Duan. 2023. Gameeval: Evaluating llms on conversational games. *CoRR*, abs/2308.10032.

Marcelo Quinderé, Luís Seabra Lopes, and António J. S. Teixeira. 2013. Evaluation of a dialogue manager for a mobile robot. In *IEEE International Symposium on Robot and Human Interactive Communication, IEEE RO-MAN 2013, Gyeongju, South Korea, August 26-29, 2013*, pages 126–132. IEEE.

Nir Ratner, Yoav Levine, Yonatan Belinkov, Ori Ram, Inbal Magar, Omri Abend, Ehud Karpas, Amnon

Shashua, Kevin Leyton-Brown, and Yoav Shoham. 2023. Parallel context windows for large language models. In *Proceedings of the 61st Annual Meeting of the Association for Computational Linguistics (Volume 1: Long Papers), ACL 2023, Toronto, Canada, July 9-14, 2023*, pages 6383–6402. Association for Computational Linguistics.

Hugo Touvron, Louis Martin, Kevin Stone, Peter Albert, Amjad Almahairi, and et al. 2023. Llama 2: Open foundation and fine-tuned chat models. *CoRR*, abs/2307.09288.

Yue Wu, Xuan Tang, Tom M. Mitchell, and Yuanzhi Li. 2023. Smartplay : A benchmark for llms as intelligent agents. *CoRR*, abs/2310.01557.

Saizheng Zhang, Emily Dinan, Jack Urbanek, Arthur Szlam, Douwe Kiela, and Jason Weston. 2018. Personalizing dialogue agents: I have a dog, do you have pets too? In *Proceedings of the 56th Annual Meeting of the Association for Computational Linguistics, ACL 2018, Melbourne, Australia, July 15-20, 2018, Volume 1: Long Papers*, pages 2204–2213. Association for Computational Linguistics.

Xuhui Zhou, Hao Zhu, Leena Mathur, Ruohong Zhang, Haofei Yu, Zhengyang Qi, Louis-Philippe Morency, Yonatan Bisk, Daniel Fried, Graham Neubig, and Maarten Sap. 2023. Sotopia: Interactive evaluation for social intelligence in language agents.

## 7 Module Prompts

The prompt templates for the baseline setup are given in Figure 3. The prompt templates for the modules are given in Figure 4 and 5.

## 8 Dialogue Transcripts

The dialogue transcripts of the *gpt-3.5-turbo* for all forms are available in Figure 10 and 11.

## 9 Forms

All four chose forms with their fields are given in Figure 6, 7, 8, and 9 for SS5 - Application for a Social Security Form [5], EPA – Report Environmental Violations [6], MED - Confidential Medical History [7], and INV - Invention Disclosure [8], respectively.

[5] https://www.ssa.gov/forms/ss-5.pdf

[6] https://echo.epa.gov/report-environmental-violations

[7] https://www.england.nhs.uk/south/wp-content/uploads/sites/6/2019/11/gwh-medical-history-forms.pdf

[8] https://researchprotections.appstate.edu/sites/researchprotections.appstate.edu/files/interactive%20ip_asu_invention%20and%20discovery%20disclosure%20form.pdf

TEMPLATE 7.0.1

**Question Generator**

```
Please generate a question. The answer to the question will be used to fill out fields of the given FORM. Try to ask about multiple fields in a single question if they are related. Give all possible Options if they are limited by the FORM. Only fields with an "answer" attribute can be filled out. Your output should be in the following format: "question": ""

FORM: [Insert 1]
```

**Form Filler**

```
Given the following ANSWER, you can do one of the following actions:
1. follow_up: Ask another question to get more information. 2. fill_form: use the answer to fill out fields in the form. 3. stop: stops the filling of the form. Only call this once all required fields have been filled.
Choose the appropriate option and output your choice in the following format: "next action": "".

ANSWER: [Insert 1]
```

Figure 3: Prompt templates used for baseline setup.

TEMPLATE 7.0.2

**Dialogue Manager**

You are managing the filling of a form by deciding what action needs to be taken. The progress can be seen in the CURRENT STATE. You can choose from the following options:

1. form_chunks: call this at the very beginning to split the form into workable chunks.
2. fill_chunk: work on a chunk of the form and fill out its fields. specify an empty chunk to work on.
3. stop: Stops the process. Call this once all chunks have been validated.

Specify what next action should be. Your output needs to have the following format: "next action": "", "chunk to work on": null

CURRENT STATE: [State]

**Chunk Filler**

You are managing the filling of a form. Based on the CURRENT STATE, decide which of the following actions should be taken:

1. "question_generation": Ask a question in order to fill out empty fields.
2. "fill_validation": validate fields that have been answered.
3. "stop": stops the filling of this form, call this once all fields are validated.

The CURRENT STATE gives you information about every field in the form. Fields can be "empty", "answered" or "validated". Only return the filled out RETURN FORM and nothing else. The output needs to have the format of the RETURN FORM.

RETURN FORM: "next action": ""

CURRENT STATE: [State]

TEMPLATE 7.0.3

**Answer Parser**

The given DIALOGUE has the goal to fill out the given FORM. You need to decide what Option should be taken next. Your options for next actions are:
1. "information_extraction": Choose this action if the given answer contains all the necessary information.
2. "follow_up_question": Choose this if the given answer is invalid or only covers part of the necessary information.
3. "repeat_question": Choose this if the User asked for clarification or did not answer the question at all.

Give your output in the following format: "next action": ""

DIALOGUE: [Insert 1]

INFORMATION TO EXTRACT: [Insert 3]

FORM: [Insert 2]

**Question Extractor**

You are given a section from a form in JSON format and are asked to summarize it into a single sentence. The section might contain multiple fields, all of which need to be part of the summary sentence. Be sure to mention if the field in the section relies on another field.
Your output should follow the following format: "summary": ""
GIVEN SECTION: [Insert]

**Question Grouping**

You are given a number of summaries which need to be grouped by their semantic commonalities. The summaries are given in the following format "name": "summary". Each summary needs to be grouped and each group contains at most 5 summaries. Choose group names based on the semantic commonalities of the summaries. The output has the following format:

"first group name": list of summary names in that group e.g. ["name of summary 3", "name of summary 2"], "second group name": list of its members e.g. ["name of summary 5"]. Only output the groups with their members without any explanation or additional information.

SUMMARIES: [Insert]

Figure 4: Prompt templates used for interactive and two task-performing modules

TEMPLATE 7.0.4

**Grouping Validator**

Given a number of summaries and a grouping of these summaries based on semantic commonalities, decide if there is a better grouping of the given summaries. If the given grouping is already the best grouping of the summaries, return the given grouping and nothing else. If there is a better way to group the summaries return the changed grouping in the same format as the original one, and nothing else, instead. Some guidelines: Each group can contain up to 5 summaries, each question needs to be grouped, group names need to be based on a common aspect of the summaries. Be sure to follow these guidelines and do not explain your answer.
SUMMARIES: [Insert 1]
GROUPING: [Insert 2]

**Question Generator**

Please generate a question. The answer to the question will be used to fill out empty fields of the given FORM. Try to ask about multiple fields in a single question if they are related. Give all possible Options if they are limited by the FORM. Only fields with an "answer" attribute can be filled out. Only ask for fields where the answer has not been given. An empty string as an answer to a field that is not required means that this field is to be left empty. Also specify which fields the question is targeted towards by listing the field names. Your output must have the following format: "question": "", "fields": []
FORM: [Insert 1]

**Follow-up Question Generator**

You are given a short dialogue and information which needs to be asked for. You are also given the form section, which the dialogue is based on. It was determined that the form can not be filled out based on the dialogue. Generate a new question in which you state what is considered a valid answer. Your output should be in the following format: "question": ""
DAILOGUE: [Insert 1]
INFORMATION TO EXTRACT: [Insert 2]
FORM SECTION: [Insert 3]

TEMPLATE 7.0.5

**Repeated Question Generator**

You are given a short dialogue and the last answer did not match what was expected. You are also given the form section, which the dialogue is based on. Your task is to write a new question that asks for the same information but also specifies what was wrong with the previous answer and nudges the User towards giving a better answer. Only return the filled out return form and nothing else.
RETURN FORM: "new question": ""
DIALOGUE: [Insert 1]
INFORMATION TO BE EXTRACTED: [Insert 2]
FORM SECTION: [Insert 3]

**Information Extractor**

You are given a short DIALOGUE. Extract information as facts about the topic discussed in the given DIALOGUE. The information needs to be stored as key, value pairs of strings of text and no other forms of data structures. Your output should have the following format: "key": "value", ... for example an acceptable output would be "day of the week": "monday", "car": "corvette"
DIALOGUE: [Insert 2]

**Form Filler**

You are given information and a section of a form in json format. You are also given the fields on which to work. If an optional field is to be left empty, write an empty string as the answer. Return the entire form section after filling out fields that have been answered.
FORM SECTION: [Insert 1]
INFORMATION: [Insert 2]
FIELDS TO WORK ON: [Insert 3]

**Answer Validator**

You are given a FORM SECTION and some INFORMATION. Please make sure that the FORM SECTION has been filled out correctly, based on the given INFORMATION. Make any changes nessecary to the FORM SECTION (if any) and return the entire FORM SECTION including your adjustments.
FORM SECTION: [Insert 1]
INFORMATION: [Insert 2]

Figure 5: Prompt templates used for task-performing modules

# Social Security SS-5 Form

**1. Name**

**1.1. Name to be shown on card.**

**1.1.1. First Name (text, required)**

**1.1.2. Full middle name (text, optional)**

**1.1.3. Last Name (text, required)**

**1.2. Full name at birth**

*Info*

These fields need to be filled out if the full name at birth is different than the Name on the Card

**1.2.1. First Name (text, required)**

**1.2.2. Full middle name (text, optional)**

**1.2.3. Last Name (text, required)**

**2. Social security number previously assigned to the person listed in item 1 (text, required)**

**3. Place of birth**

**3.1. City (text, required)**

**3.2. State or foreign country (text, required)**

**4. Date of birth (text, required)**

**5. Citizenship (single-choice, required)**

*Options*

U.S. Citizen, Legal Alien Allowed to work, Legal Alien not allowed to work, other

**6. Ethnicity – Are you Hispanic or Latino? (single-choice, optional)**

*Options*

Yes, No

**7. Race (multi-choice, required)**

*Options*

Native Hawaiian, Alaska Native, Asian, American Indian, Black/African American, Other Pacific Islander, White

**8. Sex (single-choice, required)**

*Options*

Male, Female

**9. Mother**

**9.1. Mother's Name at birth**

**9.1.1. First name (text, required)**

**9.1.2. Full middle name (text, optional)**

**9.1.3. Last name (text, required)**

**9.2. Mother's social security number (text, optional)**

**10. Father**

**10.1. Father's name at birth**

**10.1.1. First name (text, required)**

**10.1.2. Full middle name (text, optional)**

**10.1.3. Last name (text, required)**

**10.2. Father's social security number (text, optional)**

**11. Has the person listed in item 1 or anyone acting on his/her behalf ever filed for or received a social security number card before? (single-choice, required)**

*Info*

If yes, answer 12-13 else skip to 14.

Figure 6: SS5 - Application for a Social Security Form

# Environmental Violation Report Form

1. **Suspected Violator's Name (text, required)**
2. **Suspected Violation Location (text, required)**
3. **Suspected Violation City (text, required)**
4. **Suspected Violation State (text, required)**
5. **Suspected Violation ZIP Code (text, required)**
6. **Responsible Party (single-choice, required)**

*Options*
Individual, Company, Government/Military, Unknown

7. **Is the suspected Violation still occurring? (single-choice, required)**

*Options*
Yes, No

8. **Date of incident (text, required)**

*Info*
Enter Date in DD.MM.YYYY format.

9. **Is this an emergency? (single-choice, required)**

*Options*
Yes, No

10. **Intention (single-choice, required)**

*Options*
Accidental, Intentional, Unknown

11. **Violation Method (single-choice, required)**

*Options*
Release, Dump/Buried, Spill, Spray, Fill, Falsified

12. **Affected Subject(s) (single-choice, required)**

*Options*
Land, Water, Air, Worker, Documents

13. **Violation Description (text, required)**

*Info*
Include a detailed description of the violation. For example, gas drilling, drum dumping etc. If necessary, include specific directions.

14. **Reporter Contact Information**

*Info*
You are not required to provide your contact information, but the EPA might want to reach out to you for additional information.

- 14.1. **Your Name (text, optional)**
- 14.2. **Your Email (text, optional)**
- 14.3. **Your Phone Number (text, optional)**

Figure 7: EPA – Report Environmental Violations Form

# Medical Form

1. **Your Name**
   1.1. **Title (text, optional)**
   1.2. **Surname (text, required)**
   1.3. **First Name (text, required)**
2. **Your date of birth (text, required)**
3. **Your Sex (single-choice, required)**

*Options*
Male, Female

4. **Your Adress (text, required)**
5. **Your Postcode (text, required)**
6. **Your Occupation (text, required)**
7. **Your home telephone number (text, optional)**
8. **Your mobile number (text, required)**
9. **Your emergency contact**
   9.1. **Name (text, required)**
   9.2. **Phone Number (text, required)**
   9.3. **Relationship to you (text, required)**
10. **Your best interest contact**
    10.1. **Name (text, required)**
    10.2. **Phone number (text, required)**
    10.3. **Relationship to you (text, required)**
11. **Your Doctor's details**
    11.1. **Doctor's name (text, required)**
    11.2. **Doctor's Phone number (text, required)**
    11.3. **Doctor's Address (text, required)**
    11.4. **Doctor's Postcode (text, required)**
12. **Do you weigh (single-choice, required)**

*Options*
Less than 21 stone (133kg), Between 21 & 35 stone (133-222kg), more than 35 stone (222kg)

13. **Do you have (multi-choice, required)**

*Options*
Hearing Loss?, Sight Loss?, Mobility Problems?, None of the above

14. **How many units of alcohol do you drink per week? (text, required)**

*Info*
A unit is half a pint of lager, a single measure of spirits or a small glass of wine.

15. **Do you smoke tobacco products? (yes/no, required)**
16. **If you smoke tobacco products, how many daily? (text, optional)**
17. **If you don't smoke tobacco products, have you smoked in the past? (yes/no, optional)**
18. **Do you chew tobacco, pan or use gutkha? (yes/no, required)**
19. **If you do not chew tobacco, pan or use gutkha, have you done so in the past? (yes/no, optional)**
20. **Are you currently Receiving treatment from a doctor, hospital or clinic? (yes/no, required)**
21. **Are you currently Taking any prescribed medicines? (yes/no, required)**

*Info*
This includes tablets, inhalers, injections, contraceptives and ointments.

Figure 8: MED - Confidential Medical History Form

# Invention Disclosure Form

1. **What is the Title of the Invention? (text, required)**
2. **What category does the invention fall into? (single-choice, required)**

*Options*
Nano-Technology, Computational and Efficiency Enhancers, Biotechnology and Agro-medicine, Health Care/Medical Devices, Software, Manufacturing/Process Enhancers, other

*Info*
if you choose other, please answer the following question.

3. **What category would you assign to the invention? (text, optional)**
4. **Choose all categories that apply to this invention. (multi-choice, required)**

*Options*
New Process, New Device, New Product, New User of an existing Process/Product, New Composition of Matter, Improvement to an existing Process/Product

5. **When was this invention conceived? (text, required)**
6. **Describe how this invention came to be. (text, required)**
7. **Have working prototypes, product apparatus or compositions, etc. been made and tested? (single-choice, required)**

*Options*
Yes, No

8. **Give a detailed description of the Invention. (text, required)**
9. **Describe the particular problem the invention seeks to solve. (text, required)**
10. **What existing technologies or products solve or attempt to solve the same or similar problems? (text, required)**
11. **What advantage(s) does this invention provide over existing technologies or products? (text, required)**
12. **What novel and/or unusual features distinguish this invention from existing technologies or products? (text, required)**
13. **What are possible uses for the invention? (text, required)**

*Info*
List all possible commercial applications of the invention. In addition to immediate applications, are there other uses that might be realized in the future (i.e., other contemplated forms of the invention or alternate aspects/uses)?

14. **What research plans do you have for further development of the invention? (text, required)**

*Info*
Are plans in progress? Scheduled? Are plans dependent upon commercial or federal sponsorship?

Figure 9: INV - Invention Disclosure Form

CURRENT STATE: {"fields": {"1": "answered", "2": "empty", "3": "empty", "4": "empty", "5": "empty"}

Chunk Filler:
{"next action": "question_generation"}

FORM: {"2": {"Social security number previously assigned to the person listed in item 1": {"type": "number", "required": true, "answer": null, "info": "The social security number of the person specified in 1. Needs to be 9 digits long."}}, "3": {"Place of Birth": [...]}}

Question Generator:
{"question": "What is the social security number previously assigned to the person listed in item 1 "fields": ["2"]}

QUESTION: {"question": "What is the social security number previously assigned to the person listed in item 1?", "fields": ["2"]}

User:
{"answer": "I'm sorry, but as a social media influ am unable to provide the social security number person listed in item 1. It is important to protect information and keep it confidential. Please refe individual's personal records or contact the appr authorities for this information."}

DIALOGUE: [{"Assistant": "What [...] in item 1?"}, {"User": "I'm sorry, but as [...]"}] FORM: {"2": {"Social security number previously assigned to the person listed in item 1": {"type": "number", "required": true, "answer": null, "info": "The social security number of the person specified in 1. Needs to be 9 digits long}}

Answer Parser:
{"next action": "follow_up_question"}

DIALOGUE: [...] INFORMATION TO EXTRACT: ["2"] FORM: {"2": {"Social security number [...]}}

Follow-up Question Generator:
{"question": "What is the social security number previously assigned to the person listed in item 1 provide a 9-digit number as the answer."}

QUESTION: {"question": "What is the social security number previously assigned to the person listed in item 1? Please provide a 9-digit number as the answer."}

User:
{"answer": "123-45-6789"}

DIALOGUE: [{"Assistant": "What is the social [...] for this information."}, {"Assistant": "What is the social security number previously assigned to the person listed in item 1? Please provide a 9-digit number as the answer."}, {"User": "123-45-6789"}] INFORMATION TO EXTRACT: ["2"] FORM:[...]

(a) SS5 Form

CURRENT STATE: {"chunks": {}, "last action": []}

Dialogue Manager:
{"next action": "form_chunks", "chunk to work on": null}

GIVEN SECTION: {"Your Name": {"Title": {"type": "text-field", "required": false, "answer": null}, "Surname": {"type": "text-field", "required": true, "answer": null}, "First Name": {"type": "text-field", "required": true, "answer": null}}}

Question Extractor:
{"summary": "The section requires the user to provide their surname and first name, while the title field is optional."}

GIVEN SECTION: {"Your Date of Birth": {"type": "text-field", "required": true, "answer": null}}

Question Extractor:
{"summary": "The Date of Birth field is required and has not been answered."}

[...]

SUMMARIES: {"Your Name": "The section requires the user to provide their surname and first name, while the title field is optional.", "Your Date of Birth": "The Date of Birth field is required and has not been answered.", "Your Sex": "The form requires the user to select their sex from the options of male or female.", [...]"}

Question Grouping:
{"Personal Information": ["Your Name", "Your Date of Birth", "Your Sex"], "Contact Information": ["Your Address", "Your Postcode", "Your Telephone Number (home)", "Your Mobile Number", "Your emergency contact"], "Occupation Information": ["Your Occupation"]}

SUMMARIES: {"Your Name": "The section requires [...]GROUPING: {"Personal Information": ["Your Name", "Your Date of Birth", "Your Sex"], "Contact Information": ["Your Address", "Your Postcode", "Your Telephone Number (home)", "Your Mobile Number", "Your emergency contact"], "Occupation Information": ["Your Occupation"]}

Grouping Validator:
{"Personal Information": ["Your Name", "Your Date of Birth", "Your Sex"], "Contact Information": ["Your Address", "Your Postcode", "Your Telephone Number (home)", "Your Mobile Number"], "Emergency Contact Information": ["Your emergency contact"], "Occupation Information": ["Your Occupation"]}

(b) MED Form

Figure 10: Dialogue transcripts of modular setup based on *gpt-3.5-turbo* on *SS5* and *MED* forms

CURRENT STATE: {"fields": {"Is the suspected Violation still occurring?": "empty"}

Chunk Filler:
{"next action": "question_generation"}

FORM: {"Is the suspected Violation still occurring?": {"type": "checkbox", "required": true, "options": ["yes", "no"], "answer": null}}

Question Generator:
{"question": "Is the suspected Violation still occurring?", "fields": ["Is the suspected Violati occurring?"]}

QUESTION: {"question": "Is the suspected Violation still occurring?", "fields": ["Is the suspected Violation still occurring?"]}

User:
{"answer": "Yes, the suspected violation is still occ

DIALOGUE: [{"Assistant": "Is the suspected Violation still occurring?"}, {"User": "Yes, the suspected violation is still occurring."}] FORM: {"Is the suspected Violation still occurring?": {"type": "checkbox", "required": true, "options": ["yes", "no"], "answer": null}}

Answer Parser:
{"next action": "information_extraction"}

DIALOGUE: [{"Assistant": "Is the suspected Violation still occurring?"}, {"User": "Yes, the suspected violation is still occurring."}]

Information Extractor:
{"suspected violation": "still occurring"}

FORM SECTION: {"Is the suspected Violation still occurring?": {"type": "checkbox", "required": true, "options": ["yes", "no"], "answer": null}} INFORMATION: {"suspected violation": "still occurring"} FIELDS TO WORK ON: ["Is the suspected Violation still occurring?"]

Form Filler:
{ "Is the suspected Violation still occurring?": { "type": "checkbox", "required": true, "options "no"], "answer": "yes"}}

CURRENT STATE: {"fields": {"Is the suspected Violation still occurring?": "answered"}

Chunk Filler:
{"next action": "answer_validation"}

FORM SECTION: {"Is the suspected Violation still occurring?": {"type": "checkbox", "required": true, "options": ["yes", "no"], "answer": "yes"}} INFORMATION: {"suspected violation": "still occurring"}

Answer Validator:
{"Is the suspected Violation still occurring?": "checkbox", "required": true, "options": ["ye: "answer": "yes"}}

CURRENT STATE: {"fields": {"Is the suspected Violation still occurring?": "validated"}

(a) EPA Form

CURRENT STATE: {"chunks": {"Title of the Invention": "empty", "Category of the Invention": "empty", "Conception of the Invention": "empty", "Prototypes and Testing": "empty", "Description of the Invention": "empty", "Problem the Invention Seeks to Solve": "empty", "Group 1": "empty", "Group 2": "empty"}, "last action": ["form_chunks"]}

Dialogue Manager:
{"next action": "fill_chunk", "chunk to work on": "Title of the Invention"}

CURRENT STATE: {"fields": {"What is the title of the Invention?": "empty"}, "last action": [], "last question": null}

Chunk Filler:
{"next action": "question_generation"}

FORM: {"What is the title of the Invention?": {"type": "text-field", "required": true, "answer": null}}

Question Generator:
{"question": "What is the title of the Invention?", "fields": ["What is the title of the Invention?"]}

QUESTION: {"question": "What is the title of the Invention?", "fields": ["What is the title of the Invention?"]}

User:
{"answer": "The WaveTracker"}

DIALOGUE: [{"Assistant": "What is the title of the Invention?"}, {"User": "The WaveTracker"}] INFORMATION TO EXTRACT: ["What is the title of the Invention?"] FORM: {"What is the title of the Invention?": {"type": "text-field", "required": true, "answer": null}}

Answer Parser:
{"next action": "information_extraction"}

DIALOGUE: [{"Assistant": "What is the title of the Invention?"}, {"User": "The WaveTracker"}]

Information Extractor:
{"title of the Invention": "The WaveTracker"}

FORM SECTION: {"What is the title of the Invention?": {"type": "text-field", "required": true, "answer": null}} INFORMATION: {"title of the Invention": "The WaveTracker"} FIELDS TO WORK ON: ["What is the title of the Invention?"]

Form Filler:
{"What is the title of the Invention?": { "type": "text-field", "required": true,"answer": "The WaveTracker"}}

CURRENT STATE: {"fields": {"What is the title of the Invention?": "answered"}, "last action": ["question_generation"], "last question": "What is the title of the Invention?"}

(b) INV Form

Figure 11: Dialogue transcripts of the modular setup based on *gpt-3.5-turbo* on *EPA* and *INV* forms

# KAUCUS: Knowledge Augmented User Simulators for Training Language Model Assistants

**Kaustubh D. Dhole**
Department of Computer Science
Emory University
Atlanta, USA
kdhole@emory.edu

## Abstract

An effective multi-turn instruction-following assistant can be developed by creating a simulator that can generate useful interaction data. Apart from relying on its intrinsic weights, an ideal user simulator should also be able to bootstrap external knowledge rapidly in its raw form to simulate the multifarious diversity of text available over the internet. Previous user simulators generally lacked diversity, were mostly closed domain, and necessitated rigid schema making them inefficient to rapidly scale to incorporate external knowledge. In this regard, we introduce **Kaucus**, a **K**nowledge-**Au**gmented **U**ser **S**imulator framework, to outline a process of creating diverse user simulators, that can seamlessly exploit external knowledge as well as benefit downstream assistant model training. Through two GPT-J based simulators viz., a **Retrieval Augmented Simulator** and a **Summary Controlled Simulator** we generate diverse simulator-assistant interactions. Through reward and preference model-based evaluations, we find that these interactions serve as useful training data and create more helpful downstream assistants. We also find that incorporating knowledge through retrieval augmentation or summary control helps create better assistants.

## 1 Introduction

Significant advancements in Large Language Models (LLMs) have made them exceptionally adept in conversational applications like virtual assistants (Touvron et al., 2023; FitzGerald et al., 2022; OpenAI, 2023; Team et al., 2023). This proficiency is largely attributed to the notably parallelizable transformer architecture (Vaswani et al., 2017) enabling these models to utilize extensive pre-training datasets effectively (Raffel et al., 2019; Computer, 2023). To create effective assistants, LLMs are then further enhanced by learning from human interactions including popular paradigms such as RLHF (Böhm et al., 2019; Ziegler et al., 2019; Ouyang et al., 2022a). Such conversational human alignment of assistants requires large amounts of interactive dialog data, both for training as well as testing.

However, interactive data collection is a manual and slow process, particularly (a) for covering a wide range of user behaviors as well as (b) for diverse adversarial and behavior testing.

These challenges can be mitigated by simulating user behaviors by automating the generation of interactive data, reducing both time and cost, while maintaining control over the interactions. Simulated interactions can be executed at a much faster pace than manual collection efforts, limited only by the speed of inference.

Yet, current user simulators lack diversity, are mostly closed domain, and require rigid schema for control or conversation grounding. The necessity of intermediate schema in the form of a knowledge base (Kim et al., 2023) or handcrafted rules (like user persona or specific behaviors) while being excellent drivers to ground conversations, make it hard to develop scalable simulators – that can utilize natural text freely available on the internet and rapidly create corresponding assistant models. A simulator should be able to exploit external knowledge rapidly and also be controllable without a rigid schema. We argue that such a knowledge simulator can be helpful in two ways – It can seamlessly convert free-form text to useful training data without user intervention as well as provide a natural control to direct simulators for specific behaviors (Mille et al., 2021; Cheng et al., 2023).

Hence, in this work, we propose **Kaucus**, a **K**nowledge **Au**gmented **S**imulator Framework[1]. Through this framework, we demonstrate the usage of external sources of knowledge – viz. Retrieval Augmentation and Summary Control – for creating

[1]pronounced like Caucus derived from Algonquian cau'-cau'-as'u meaning 'adviser'



*Proceedings of the 1st Workshop on Simulating Conversational Intelligence in Chat (SCI-CHAT 2024)*, pages 53–65
March 21, 2024 ©2024 Association for Computational Linguistics

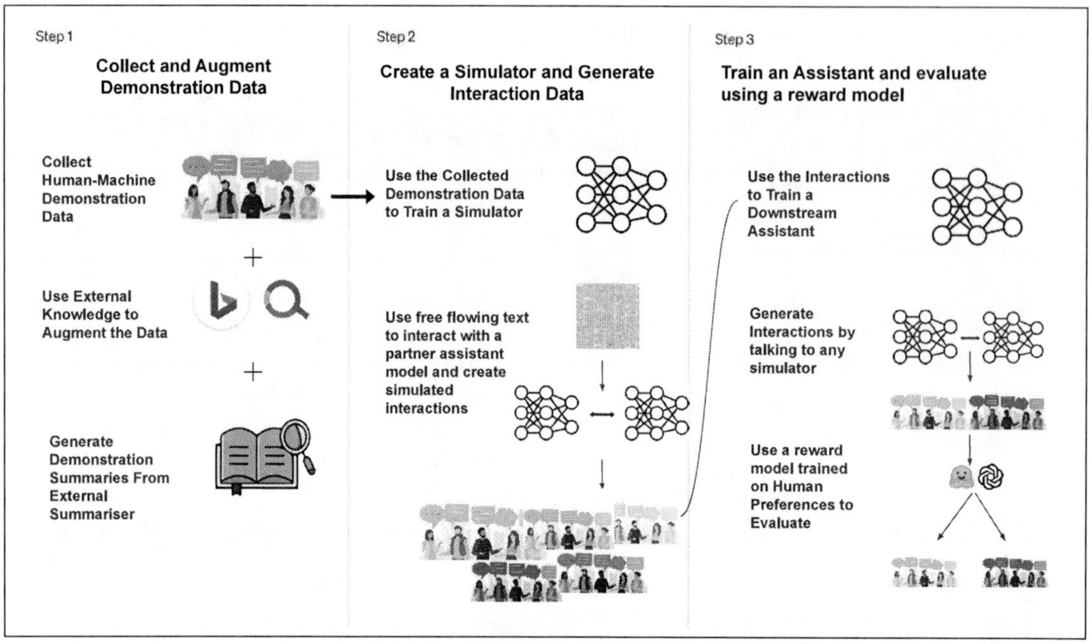


Figure 1: The complete three step framework of **Kaucus** – creating, utilizing and evaluating a user simulator.

user simulators that can incorporate free-flowing text and result in better assistant training.

The paper is organized as follows: In Section 2, we first discuss existing work related to user simulators. In Section 3, we define simulators and introduce **Kaucus**, through two knowledge simulators. We further describe the efficacy of each through training and evaluating downstream assistant models. Our retrieval augmented simulator, **SRAG** shows how retrieving relevant passages with a simple BM25 retriever can be used to improve intrinsic metrics as well as provide useful training data to train helpful assistants. We also introduce the summary-controlled setting, **SCTRL** to build scalable simulators to exploit freely available text and further measure their performance with and without retrieval.

## 2 Related Work

User simulators have been studied in various settings. Aher et al. (2023) create four simulators that elicit behavior to judge an assistant's fairness, rationality, grammaticality, and general knowledge, and then measure them qualitatively. Their simulators are models with different prompt templates. Training multi-agent interactions has been a popular choice in reinforcement learning. Horton (2023); Argyle et al. (2023) create simulations for economic purposes by endowing GPT3 (Brown et al., 2020) with demographic characteristics and then get responses in various scenarios that match what is seen empirically. Irving et al. (2018) in AI safety has proposed using self-play and self-debate to train AI agents to pursue human goals and preferences. Two tasks in the collaborative benchmark, BIG-Bench (Srivastava et al., 2023) evaluate the model's ability for self-evaluation by simulating specific human professions. They make the models to act as lawyers, tutors[2], judges[3], students, etc. and then have separate model instances to evaluate the conversation. Each of the roles is invoked by user-specific prompts like "You are a lawyer" and a subsequent model-based evaluation is performed by prompting to seek numerical ratings.

Kreyssig et al. (2018)'s Neural User Simulations involve training encoder-decoder RNNs on dialogues between real users and a spoken dialogue system (SDS) in a restaurant domain and then using the trained simulator to train the policy of a reinforcement learning based SDS. They further use Schatzmann et al. (2005)'s cross-model evaluation to compare user simulators by training different policies with each simulator and testing it with other simulators. Gur et al. (2018) encode dialog history and a goal to generate user responses for task-oriented dialog. Kraus et al. (2023a); Li et al.

[2]BIG-Bench Self Evaluation Tutoring
[3]BIG-Bench Self Evaluation Courtroom

(2022b) prompt LLMs with task-oriented dialog data, such as goals, and perform intrinsic evaluation over the generated data to show the effectiveness of their approaches. Kim et al. (2023) generate conversations grounded on common sense by prompting InstructGPT with knowledge base triples. Their human evaluations show that oftentimes humans prefer model outputs against their human-written counterparts. Liu et al. (2023) leverage multiple user simulators to train task-oriented dialog systems. Faltings et al. (2023) utilize user simulators that offer edits to guide the model towards achieving a specified target text training them using Imitation Learning.

Other studies augment simulators with emotions (Lin et al., 2023) and trusting behaviours (Kraus et al., 2023b). For instance, Lin et al. (2023) simulate user emotions alongside user behavior based on the user goal, the dialogue history, and persona. Giabbanelli (2023) utilize GPT-based models for scientific simulations while Schaefer et al. (2023) explore LLMs to simulate biological systems.

With the popularity of large language models deployed in closed-source settings, bootstrapping training data from them has become useful. Taori et al. (2023) create downstream assistant models by training LLama-7B and 13B models (Touvron et al., 2023) on 52K single-turn instruction following demonstrations generated through self-instruct (Wang et al., 2023b) from `text-davinci-003` (Brown et al., 2020). Bian et al. (2023) create a dialog corpus by extending the same to the multi-turn setting. Dai et al. (2022) show improved conversation retrieval by proposing a mechanism to convert Wikipedia passages to dialog.

On the other hand, retrieval augmentation has been the focus of many recent efforts (Schick et al., 2023; Zhang et al., 2023; Wang et al., 2023a; Li et al., 2022a) as it offers advantages such as up-to-date information access beyond an LLM's training dataset, incorporation of proprietary or domain-specific data at runtime, and enhanced factuality in outputs compared to standard LLMs. Studies have been performed by training RAG systems end-to-end (Guu et al., 2020; Lewis et al., 2020) as well as using retrieval in context for various tasks (Ram et al., 2023; Jiang et al., 2023; Gao et al., 2023; Dhole and Agichtein, 2024).

## 3 The Kaucus Framework

In this section, we introduce **Kaucus**, a 3-stage framework, and outline the process of creating knowledge-augmented simulators as shown in Figure 1. Our approach involves the following steps:

### 3.1 Data Collection and Augmentation

We start by gathering interaction data – essentially conversations between a user and a base assistant LLM, which will be later augmented to enrich the training process. For instance, the base LLM could take the form of closed-source instruct models such as OpenAI's GPT-4, Claude, or BingChat which are widely used for work.

### 3.2 Training a Language Model (LM) as a Simulator

The next step involves training a Language Model (LM) to act as a simulator. This LM can then serve as a conversation generator for data augmentation (Dhole et al., 2023) or be integrated into a pipeline that relies on conversation interactions, such as Reinforcement Learning from Human Feedback (RLHF) (Ziegler et al., 2019; Ouyang et al., 2022b). Our work focuses on the former.

### 3.3 Leveraging the User Simulator

Once the user simulator is trained, there are several methods to utilize for improving an assistant Language Model (LM). Our work resorts to data augmentation, which will be the focus of our second set of experiments. It involves using the user simulator to generate additional training data to enhance the assistant LM's performance.

### 3.4 Evaluation

To evaluate the effectiveness of the user simulator, we will employ both intrinsic and extrinsic metrics. Intrinsic metrics will be measured over the interactions with the simulator, assessing its performance in generating relevant and coherent responses. On the other hand, extrinsic metrics will be based on evaluating a downstream assistant model trained over these interactions, which will help us gauge the impact of the user simulator on overall assistant performance. We will describe the evaluation in detail in Section 5.

## 4 Methods and Experiments

We now specifically describe the two types of knowledge-augmented simulators, viz. Utterance

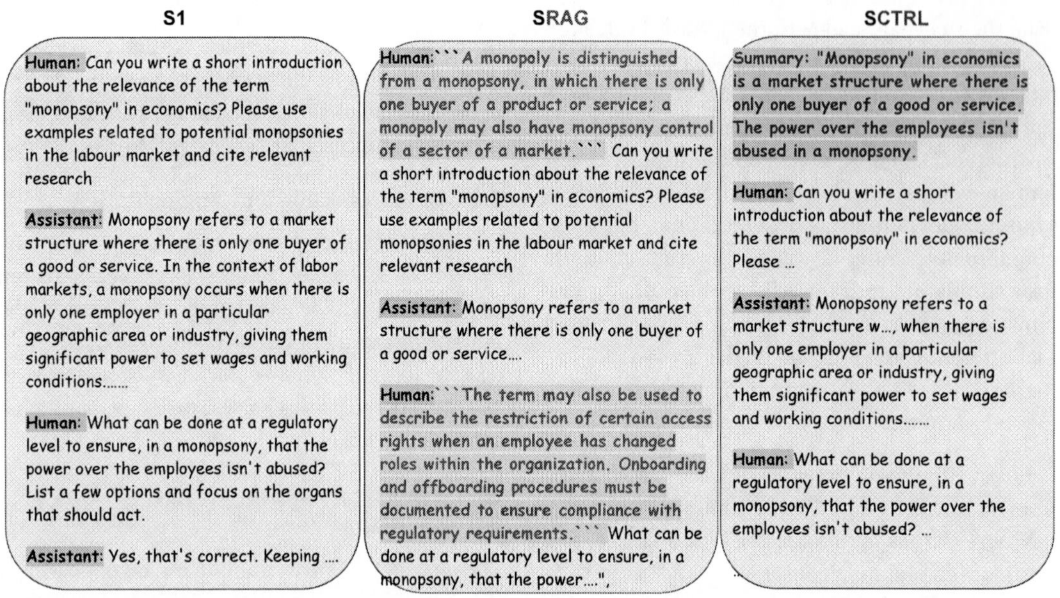


Figure 2: The format of the conversations used for training S1 (a vanilla simulator), SRAG (retrieved document shown in green), and SCTRL (summary shown in red).

Grounded Simulators (S1 and SRAG) and Summary Controlled Simulators (SCTRL).

### 4.1 Utterance Grounded Simulators

Here we train simulators with human-machine demonstration data by feeding models the conversation history to create simulators that can be triggered from a starting utterance. We create two simulators – S1 and SRAG by fine-tuning an unsupervised pre-trained GPJ-6B (Wang and Komatsuzaki, 2021) model. We describe the training process for both below:

#### 4.1.1 S1

Simulator Trained on Anthropic and Open Assistant Conversations

- **Training Data**: For training S1, we use demonstration data available through Open Assistant's conversations (Köpf et al., 2023) and Anthropic's helpful splits (Bai et al., 2022).
- **Format**: The Simulator's training data consists of `(context, human-response)` pairs. For every "Human" utterance in all the conversations, we select all the previous utterances along with their speaker information and pass it as an input to the model. The input also consists of a "Human:" string at the end. The associated human response is passed as the output.

#### 4.1.2 SRAG

**Retrieval Augmented Simulator** Trained on Anthropic and Open Assistant Conversations with BM25 Retrieval on MSMarco

Simulators could benefit from the incorporation of external knowledge which can be helpful to steer the conversation, improve factuality and most importantly introduce variation. To test our hypothesis, we train the second simulator, SRAG by incorporating passages retrieved from an external retriever.

- **Training Data**: We augment the interactions used to train S1 with passage snippets from the MS-Marco dataset (Nguyen et al., 2016; Bajaj et al., 2016), which is a large-scale dataset of 8.8M passages popularly used for information retrieval and reading comprehension. Having been generated from real users' search queries, it provides a vast repository of documents collected on a plethora of topics over the web.
- **Format**: We use `(context, human-response)` pairs in the style of S1 with human turns annotated with retrieved MSMarco passages. Using the human

utterance as a query, we execute a BM25 retriever against an MSMarco Passage Index for every human turn. Each of the human utterances is then prepended with a retrieved passage as shown in Figure 2 in green. We use the MSMarco index provided by IRDatasets (MacAvaney et al., 2021) and the BM25 implementation provided by PyTerrier (Macdonald et al., 2021).

### 4.2 Summary Controlled Simulators

The previous utterance-grounded setting relies on a conversational utterance at inference time to initiate the interaction. While it can be easy to obtain such conversational utterances using existing conversational datasets, they can quickly become scarce and out-of-date. It would be of interest to be able to scale over vast amounts of free text available over the web. However, most of the web data exists in a non-conversational format unsuitable for direct incorporation in the training process.

**SCTRL**: In that regard, we introduce the training of **summary controlled simulators** that can utilize the conversational summary obtained from an external conversation summarizer during training. This can be potentially helpful in two ways – It can provide a mechanism for the simulator to attempt to seamlessly convert "free form text" to "interaction data" while also coming up with the "simulator trigger" by itself reducing our reliance on conversational corpora. As compared to a fixed schema or a knowledge base, it can provide a natural control to guide simulators for specific behaviors via natural language texts which are generally available in plenty as compared to their conversational or interactive counterparts.

- **Training Data**: To create the training data, we append a conversational summary generated from an external conversational summarizer, at the beginning of the conversation. Our objective is to force the simulator to be able to learn the association between the initial non-conversational text and the subsequent conversation. We choose an existing BART Summariser (Wolf et al., 2020) fine-tuned on various dialog and non-dialog summarisation datasets like DialogSum, AMI and XSUM.

- **Format**: We prepend the predicted summary at the start of the conversation as shown in Figure 2 in red.

We create the two summary-controlled counterparts of S1 and SRAG as SCTRL and SCTRL-RAG respectively.

**SCTRL-RAG** Summary Controlled Simulator Trained on Anthropic and Open Assistant Conversations with MSMarco BM25 Retrieval

We use a GPT-J-6B model RLHF fine-tuned on demonstration data as our base assistant model and our simulator. We use deepspeed (Rasley et al., 2020) to optimize training and train for 10 epochs on a learning rate of $10^{-6}$.

## 5 Evaluation & Results

### 5.1 Intrinsic Metrics

We first seek to assess the "diversity" of the generated interactions. In assessing diversity, we utilize well-established reference-free lexical metrics viz. TTR, logTTR, RootTTR, HDD, and MTLD are based on type-token ratios and are quick to compute. The Measure of Textual Lexical Diversity (MTLD) is a prevalent and contemporary TTR metric that does not vary as a function of text length and explains textual information that similar lexical diversity approaches do not account for (McCarthy and Jarvis, 2010). It gauges the proportion of distinct word stems (types) to the overall word count (tokens). HDD is an alternative metric that captures additionally unique lexical information (McCarthy and Jarvis, 2010)[4].

We first generate 125 interactions by making each of the simulators interact with a fixed assistant model. The conversation is initialized with an existing Anthropic conversation in the case of S1 and SRAG and five more turns are generated (referred to as the augmented length). In SCTRL and SCTRL-RAG, 5 turns are generated from scratch from Anthropic's conversation summary. We present the results in Table 2. The metrics measure the lexical diversity only on the utterances generated via the simulator interaction (and not on the initial Anthropic conversation history that was fed to initiate the interaction). Across all metrics, incorporating a knowledge component, through retrieval augmentation (SRAG) or summary control (SCTRL) improves diversity. Incorporating both improves diversity across RootTTR and HDD metrics.

[4] Through a separate ancillary study, we also find that simulators trained on dialog data generate more diverse text as compared to pre-trained ones according to the above metrics.

| Source | Type | Generated Interaction Data | Assistant |
|---|---|---|---|
| Human | – | Assistant Trained With Anthropic_8k | A0 |
| S1 | Without Knowledge | Simulated Anthropic_8k | A1 |
| SRAG | With Retrieval Augmentation | Simulated Anthropic_8k + MSMarco | A1-RAG |
| S1-CTRL | With Summary Control | Simulated Anthropic_8k*10 summaries | A1-CTRL |
| S1-CTRL-RAG | Both | Simulated Anthropic_8k*10 summaries + MSMarco | A1-CTRL-RAG |

Table 1: The sources of various simulated data used in **Kaucus** to train the corresponding assistants

| Simulator | MTLD | Root TTR | LogTTR | HDD |
|---|---|---|---|---|
| **S1** | 23.177 | 2.918 | 0.818 | 0.04 |
| **SRAG** | **24.632** | **3.223** | **0.82** | **0.134** |
| **SCTRL** | **25.864** | **3.437** | **0.844** | **0.131** |
| **SCTRL-RAG** | 22.761 | 2.976 | 0.766 | 0.278 |

Table 2: Lexical diversity metrics on 125 conversations of each simulator. The top-2 highly diverse simulators are the knowledge-based ones - SRAG and SCTRL on all metrics.

## 5.2 Extrinsic Metrics

Although the aforementioned metrics can assist in evaluating and comparing various user simulators as potential data augmenters and generators, it is crucial to determine if they benefit subsequent assistant models. The RLHF paradigm, by training reward models, has demonstrated assistants that are more helpful, honest, and less harmful providing a promising direction for aligning with human preferences. In this regard, we resort to the family of reward and preference models to measure how well assistant models trained using data produced from various simulators perform.

**Training Downstream Assistant Models**: For each simulator trained (S1, SRAG,..), we create a subsequent assistant model (A1, ARAG, ...) and use reward modeling to measure the helpfulness of each of the assistant models. To create training data for each of the assistant models, we first simulate interactions between the corresponding simulator model along a separately held-out assistant model.

For each utterance grounded simulator (S1 and SRAG), we use 8000 Anthropic conversations as triggers. Particularly, we utilize the complete Anthropic conversation as the starting history for both the simulator and the separately held-out assistant model and allow ten turns (5 pairs) of interactions to be generated. Using the simulator to generate longer contexts provides an opportunity to collect a larger number of `(context, assistant-response)` pairs for training the downstream assistant model.

For the retrieval augmented simulator, SRAG, it is necessary to retrieve passages relevant to the ongoing conversation. We hence use the previous assistant response as a query to our MSMarco Passage Index before generating the simulator turn. The top-ranked passage via BM25 is then placed at the end of the input to SRAG.

For generating interactions from SCTRL, we need free-flowing text as the initial trigger. We generate 8000 conversations from conversation summaries of the Anthropic dataset. We use additional 9*8K passages from MS-Marco as initial triggers to act as implicit summaries.

After generating the conversations, we convert them into `(context, assistant-response)` pairs and use them as training data for predicting the assistant response given all the previous utterances. We call the subsequent assistant models A1, ARAG and ACTRL. The training details of each assistant model are described in Table 1.

**Baseline**: We additionally train an assistant model, A0 using raw 8000 conversations from Anthropic to act as appropriate baseline.

**Test Set**: For evaluation, we utilize 200 utterances from the test set of Anthropic's dataset.

**FastChat Evaluation**: FastChat (Zheng et al., 2023) is a platform for evaluating and serving LLMs. We resort to FastChat evaluation for prompting GPT-4 (OpenAI, 2023) for a comparative evaluation between two simulators. The process involves GPT-4 being input with two conversations, placed one after the other, along with an instruction to evaluate and generate a numerical score. We attribute a win, a loss, or a tie depending on whether the first (assistant model on the left in all the images) has a value greater, lesser, or equal to the second (one on the right).

**SteamSHP Reward Model Evaluation** SteamSHP-XL (Ethayarajh et al., 2022) is a preference model fine-tuned on top of an instruction-tuned model FLAN-T5-XL (Wei et al.; Longpre et al., 2023) to predict which response humans will find more helpful, given some context and two possible responses. On being prompted the same context, the reward model setting compares the probabilities assigned independently to each model response to infer the preference label.

**SteamSHP Preference Model Evaluation** (Ethayarajh et al., 2022) Preference modeling, like the FastChat Evaluation, compares two model responses through a single inference pass, which can be used to compute the probability of the first one being better than the second.

To avoid any bias occurring through the order of two conversations, we also calculate the scores with the simulator order reversed in the prompt.

For each plot, the columns indicate the two assistant models being compared. The colors in blue for each row indicate when the evaluation system prefers the left-hand side model as compared to the right-hand side when compared against A0.

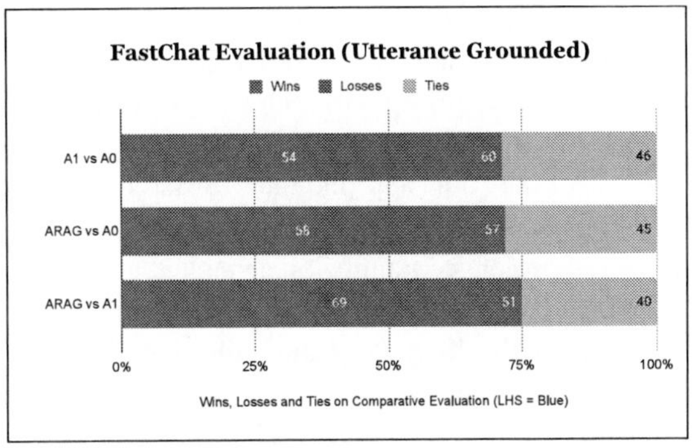


Figure 3: FastChat Evaluation of Assistants created from Utterance Grounded Simulators (A1 and ARAG) against baseline assistant (A0)

**Effect of Simulator:** We first compare A1 (i.e. the assistant trained on 8k interactions generated from S1) against A0 (i.e. the one trained without the help of the simulator). A1 outperforms A0 in all three evaluations as seen on the first rows of Figures 3, 5 and 7. The results are more prominent in SteamSHP's evaluations. This shows that with the help of a simulator, we can generate more data and improve downstream assistant performance.

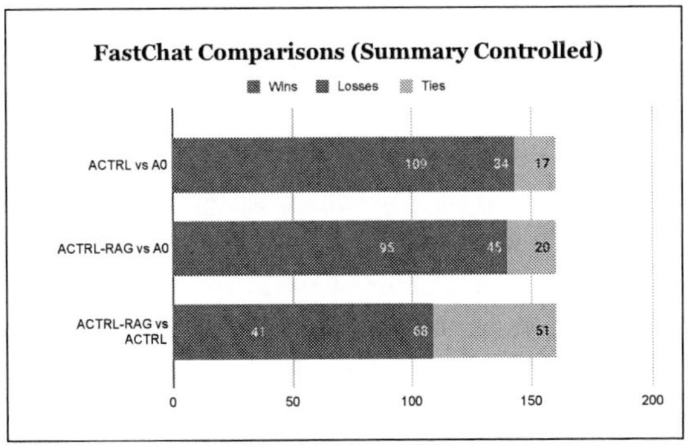


Figure 4: FastChat Evaluation of Assistants created from Summary Controlled Simulators (-CTRL) against baseline assistant (A0)

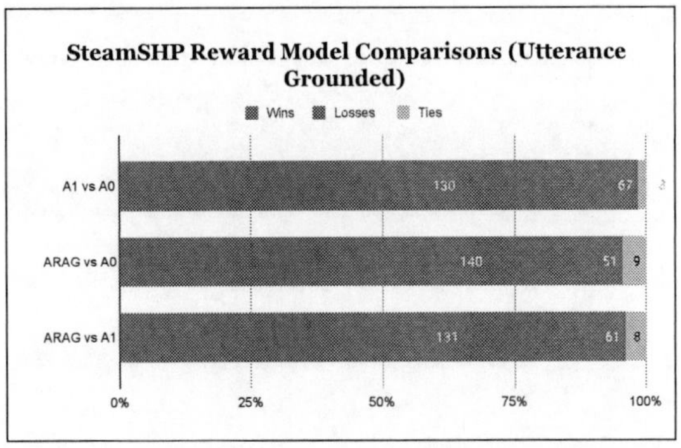


Figure 5: SteamSHP reward model Evaluation of Assistants created from Utterance Grounded against baseline assistant (A0)

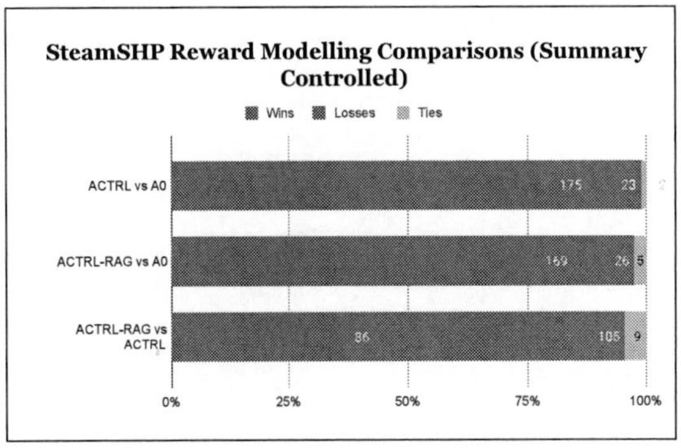


Figure 6: SteamSHP reward model Evaluation of Assistants created from Summary Controlled Simulators (-CTRL) against baseline assistant (A0)

**Effect of Retrieval Augmentation:** We then compare whether an assistant model ARAG, trained from retrieval augmented data benefits training. With the retrieval augmented simulator, downstream performance across all metrics is improved. ARAG's interactions are preferred more often as compared to A0 as well as A1 as seen in the 2nd and 3rd rows of Figures 3, 5 and 7.

**Effect of Summary Control:** The assistants ACTRL and ACTRL-RAG trained from the summary-controlled simulators are more often preferred across all the evaluations as shown in the first two rows of Figures 4, 6 and 8. However, the non-retrieval counterpart ACTRL is more often preferred as compared to the retrieval counterpart.

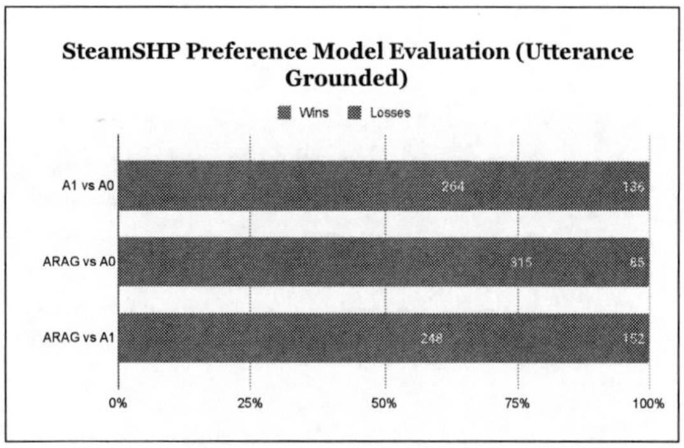


Figure 7: SteamSHP Preference model Evaluation of Assistants created from Utterance Grounded Simulators against baseline assistant (A0)

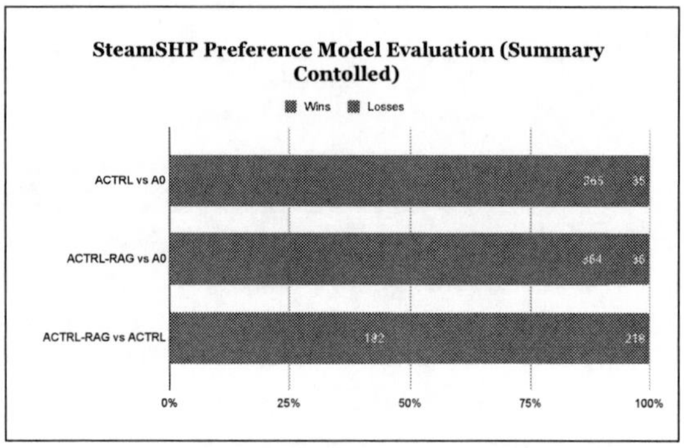


Figure 8: SteamSHP Preference model Evaluation of Assistants created from Summary Controlled (-CTRL) against baseline assistant (A0)

## 6 Conclusion

Simulators provide a way to generate data to create downstream assistant models saving human time and effort. Through our framework **Kaucus**, we further showed that augmenting simulators by exploiting external knowledge helps generate diverse interactions and as well as creates more helpful assistants than vanilla simulators. We describe two types of knowledge-augmented simulators, a Retrieval Augmented Simulator, SRAG, and a summary-controlled simulator, SCTRL both of which consume external knowledge in unique ways.

Raw text is more prevalent than the conversational counterparts. Controlling simulators through conversational summaries or external documents can be a quick and powerful tool to convert public text to trainable interaction data and create more helpful assistants. It provisions the simulator to generate interactions for novel information outside the scope of an LLM's intrinsic parameters. We hope **Kaucus** will help encourage the development of automated techniques to be able to incorporate the vast amount of text produced rapidly over the internet and align assistant models better with newer data as well as be able to control the distribution of training data without the need for a rigid schema.

## Limitations

Retrieval Augmentation helps incorporate diversity as well as benefit downstream models. We chose to use BM25 as our choice of retriever. However, there are dense retrievers (Khattab and Zaharia, 2020) and neural rerankers (Pradeep et al., 2023) that perform better than BM25 across a range of information retrieval benchmarks. Our focus was to show the benefit of incorporating external knowledge while performing a rigorous set of experiments with the same. Future studies could specifically study the impact of additional hyperparameter tuning by using varied choices of the retriever, the retrieving query, choice of summarisers and also gauge the impact of different domains than those of the Anthropic and the MSMarco datasets.

Besides, our study does not consider the impact of prolonged training on generated data which could cause potential problems of model forgetting over the long run (Shumailov et al., 2023). More experiments conducted to gauge long-term viability would shed better light on the efficacy of knowledge simulators.

All the evaluations conducted in this paper were automated – through popular reward or preference models. Human evaluations can provide better additional insights. Besides, the current intrinsic metrics primarily focus on diversity, which, while important, is only one dimension of dialogue evaluation and future work would benefit from other measures depending on the application.

## Ethics Statement

Our study has focused on the benefits of employing simulators to improve downstream assistant models. We believe that these simulators can also act as effective testers of assistants to pre-encounter and regurgitate harmful or undesirable assistant content before assistant models are deployed in impacting end applications. We should maintain caution against their unethical usage or if such regurgitation is exploited to cause harm. Just like assistants or other applications of large language models (Dhole, 2023), simulators should also be gauged from a socio-technical lens, and appropriate checks and fallback mechanisms should be employed before their actual usage. Besides, simulators themselves could inadvertently learn biases in the training data, leading to unfair or biased generations, and can be exploited for malicious purposes such as generating fake news and harmful content or asking triggering questions.

## Acknowledgements

The author would like to thank the three anonymous reviewers for their useful suggestions.

## References

Gati V Aher, Rosa I Arriaga, and Adam Tauman Kalai. 2023. Using large language models to simulate multiple humans and replicate human subject studies. In *International Conference on Machine Learning*, pages 337–371. PMLR.

Lisa P Argyle, Ethan C Busby, Nancy Fulda, Joshua R Gubler, Christopher Rytting, and David Wingate. 2023. Out of one, many: Using language models to simulate human samples. *Political Analysis*, 31(3):337–351.

Yuntao Bai, Andy Jones, Kamal Ndousse, Amanda Askell, Anna Chen, Nova DasSarma, Dawn Drain, Stanislav Fort, Deep Ganguli, Tom Henighan, et al. 2022. Training a helpful and harmless assistant with reinforcement learning from human feedback. *arXiv preprint arXiv:2204.05862*.

Payal Bajaj, Daniel Campos, Nick Craswell, Li Deng, Jianfeng Gao, Xiaodong Liu, Rangan Majumder, Andrew McNamara, Bhaskar Mitra, Tri Nguyen, et al. 2016. Ms marco: A human generated machine reading comprehension dataset. *arXiv preprint arXiv:1611.09268*.

Ning Bian, Hongyu Lin, Yaojie Lu, Xianpei Han, Le Sun, and Ben He. 2023. Chatalpaca: A multi-turn dialogue corpus based on alpaca instructions. https://github.com/cascip/ChatAlpaca.

Florian Böhm, Yang Gao, Christian M. Meyer, Ori Shapira, Ido Dagan, and Iryna Gurevych. 2019. Better rewards yield better summaries: Learning to summarise without references. In *Proceedings of the 2019 Conference on Empirical Methods in Natural Language Processing and the 9th International Joint Conference on Natural Language Processing (EMNLP-IJCNLP)*, pages 3110–3120, Hong Kong, China. Association for Computational Linguistics.

Tom Brown, Benjamin Mann, Nick Ryder, Melanie Subbiah, Jared D Kaplan, Prafulla Dhariwal, Arvind Neelakantan, Pranav Shyam, Girish Sastry, Amanda Askell, et al. 2020. Language models are few-shot learners. *Advances in neural information processing systems*, 33:1877–1901.

Myra Cheng, Tiziano Piccardi, and Diyi Yang. 2023. CoMPosT: Characterizing and evaluating caricature in LLM simulations. In *Proceedings of the 2023 Conference on Empirical Methods in Natural Language Processing*, pages 10853–10875, Singapore. Association for Computational Linguistics.

Together Computer. 2023. Redpajama: An open source recipe to reproduce llama training dataset.

Zhuyun Dai, Arun Tejasvi Chaganty, Vincent Zhao, Aida Amini, Mike Green, Qazi Rashid, and Kelvin Guu. 2022. Dialog inpainting: Turning documents to dialogs. In *International Conference on Machine Learning (ICML)*. PMLR.

Kaustubh Dhole. 2023. Large language models as SocioTechnical systems. In *Proceedings of the Big Picture Workshop*, pages 66–79, Singapore, Singapore. Association for Computational Linguistics.

Kaustubh Dhole and Eugene Agichtein. 2024. Genqrensemble : Zero-shot llm ensemble prompting for generative query reformulation. In *Advances in Information Retrieval*.

Kaustubh Dhole, Varun Gangal, Sebastian Gehrmann, Aadesh Gupta, Zhenhao Li, Saad Mahamood, Abinaya Mahadiran, Simon Mille, Ashish Shrivastava, Samson Tan, et al. 2023. Nl-augmenter: A framework for task-sensitive natural language augmentation. *Northern European Journal of Language Technology*, 9(1).

Kawin Ethayarajh, Yejin Choi, and Swabha Swayamdipta. 2022. Understanding dataset difficulty with $\mathcal{V}$-usable information. In *Proceedings of the 39th International Conference on Machine Learning*, volume 162 of *Proceedings of Machine Learning Research*, pages 5988–6008. PMLR.

Felix Faltings, Michel Galley, Kianté Brantley, Baolin Peng, Weixin Cai, Yizhe Zhang, Jianfeng Gao, and Bill Dolan. 2023. Interactive text generation. In *Proceedings of the 2023 Conference on Empirical Methods in Natural Language Processing*, pages 4450–4468, Singapore. Association for Computational Linguistics.

Jack FitzGerald, Shankar Ananthakrishnan, Konstantine Arkoudas, Davide Bernardi, Abhishek Bhagia, Claudio Delli Bovi, Jin Cao, Rakesh Chada, Amit Chauhan, Luoxin Chen, Anurag Dwarakanath, Satyam Dwivedi, Turan Gojayev, Karthik Gopalakrishnan, Thomas Gueudre, Dilek Hakkani-Tur, Wael Hamza, Jonathan J. Hüser, Kevin Martin Jose, Haidar Khan, Beiye Liu, Jianhua Lu, Alessandro Manzotti, Pradeep Natarajan, Karolina Owczarzak, Gokmen Oz, Enrico Palumbo, Charith Peris, Chandana Satya Prakash, Stephen Rawls, Andy Rosenbaum, Anjali Shenoy, Saleh Soltan, Mukund Harakere Sridhar, Lizhen Tan, Fabian Triefenbach, Pan Wei, Haiyang Yu, Shuai Zheng, Gokhan Tur, and Prem Natarajan. 2022. Alexa teacher model: Pretraining and distilling multi-billion-parameter encoders for natural language understanding systems. In *Proceedings of the*

*28th ACM SIGKDD Conference on Knowledge Discovery and Data Mining*, KDD '22, page 2893–2902, New York, NY, USA. Association for Computing Machinery.

Luyu Gao, Zhuyun Dai, Panupong Pasupat, Anthony Chen, Arun Tejasvi Chaganty, Yicheng Fan, Vincent Zhao, Ni Lao, Hongrae Lee, Da-Cheng Juan, et al. 2023. Rarr: Researching and revising what language models say, using language models. In *Proceedings of the 61st Annual Meeting of the Association for Computational Linguistics (Volume 1: Long Papers)*, pages 16477–16508.

Philippe J Giabbanelli. 2023. Gpt-based models meet simulation: How to efficiently use large-scale pre-trained language models across simulation tasks. *arXiv preprint arXiv:2306.13679*.

Izzeddin Gur, Semih Yavuz, Yu Su, and Xifeng Yan. 2018. DialSQL: Dialogue based structured query generation. In *Proceedings of the 56th Annual Meeting of the Association for Computational Linguistics (Volume 1: Long Papers)*, pages 1339–1349, Melbourne, Australia. Association for Computational Linguistics.

Kelvin Guu, Kenton Lee, Zora Tung, Panupong Pasupat, and Ming-Wei Chang. 2020. Realm: Retrieval-augmented language model pre-training. *ArXiv*, abs/2002.08909.

John J Horton. 2023. Large language models as simulated economic agents: What can we learn from homo silicus? Technical report, National Bureau of Economic Research.

Geoffrey Irving, Paul Christiano, and Dario Amodei. 2018. Ai safety via debate. *arXiv preprint arXiv:1805.00899*.

Zhengbao Jiang, Frank Xu, Luyu Gao, Zhiqing Sun, Qian Liu, Jane Dwivedi-Yu, Yiming Yang, Jamie Callan, and Graham Neubig. 2023. Active retrieval augmented generation. In *Proceedings of the 2023 Conference on Empirical Methods in Natural Language Processing*, pages 7969–7992, Singapore. Association for Computational Linguistics.

Omar Khattab and Matei Zaharia. 2020. Colbert: Efficient and effective passage search via contextualized late interaction over bert. In *Proceedings of the 43rd International ACM SIGIR conference on research and development in Information Retrieval*, pages 39–48.

Hyunwoo Kim, Jack Hessel, Liwei Jiang, Peter West, Ximing Lu, Youngjae Yu, Pei Zhou, Ronan Le Bras, Malihe Alikhani, Gunhee Kim, Maarten Sap, and Yejin Choi. 2023. Soda: Million-scale dialogue distillation with social commonsense contextualization.

Andreas Köpf, Yannic Kilcher, Dimitri von Rütte, Sotiris Anagnostidis, Zhi Rui Tam, Keith Stevens, Abdullah Barhoum, Duc Minh Nguyen, Oliver Stanley, Richárd Nagyfi, Shahul ES, Sameer Suri, David Alexandrovich Glushkov, Arnav Varma Dantuluri, Andrew Maguire, Christoph Schuhmann, Huu Nguyen, and Alexander Julian Mattick. 2023. Openassistant conversations - democratizing large language model alignment. In *Thirty-seventh Conference on Neural Information Processing Systems Datasets and Benchmarks Track*.

Matthias Kraus, Ron Riekenbrauck, and Wolfgang Minker. 2023a. Development of a trust-aware user simulator for statistical proactive dialog modeling in human-ai teams. In *Adjunct Proceedings of the 31st ACM Conference on User Modeling, Adaptation and Personalization*, pages 38–43.

Matthias Kraus, Ron Riekenbrauck, and Wolfgang Minker. 2023b. Development of a trust-aware user simulator for statistical proactive dialog modeling in human-ai teams. In *Adjunct Proceedings of the 31st ACM Conference on User Modeling, Adaptation and Personalization*, pages 38–43.

Florian Kreyssig, Iñigo Casanueva, Paweł Budzianowski, and Milica Gašić. 2018. Neural user simulation for corpus-based policy optimisation of spoken dialogue systems. In *Proceedings of the 19th Annual SIGdial Meeting on Discourse and Dialogue*, pages 60–69, Melbourne, Australia. Association for Computational Linguistics.

Patrick Lewis, Ethan Perez, Aleksandra Piktus, Fabio Petroni, Vladimir Karpukhin, Naman Goyal, Heinrich Küttler, Mike Lewis, Wen-tau Yih, Tim Rocktäschel, et al. 2020. Retrieval-augmented generation for knowledge-intensive nlp tasks. *Advances in Neural Information Processing Systems*, 33:9459–9474.

Huayang Li, Yixuan Su, Deng Cai, Yan Wang, and Lemao Liu. 2022a. A survey on retrieval-augmented text generation. *arXiv preprint arXiv:2202.01110*.

Zekun Li, Wenhu Chen, Shiyang Li, Hong Wang, Jing Qian, and Xifeng Yan. 2022b. Controllable dialogue simulation with in-context learning. In *Findings of the Association for Computational Linguistics: EMNLP 2022*, pages 4330–4347, Abu Dhabi, United Arab Emirates. Association for Computational Linguistics.

Hsien-Chin Lin, Shutong Feng, Christian Geishauser, Nurul Lubis, Carel van Niekerk, Michael Heck, Benjamin Ruppik, Renato Vukovic, and Milica Gasić. 2023. Emous: Simulating user emotions in task-oriented dialogues. SIGIR '23, page 2526–2531, New York, NY, USA. Association for Computing Machinery.

Yajiao Liu, Xin Jiang, Yichun Yin, Yasheng Wang, Fei Mi, Qun Liu, Xiang Wan, and Benyou Wang. 2023. One cannot stand for everyone! leveraging multiple user simulators to train task-oriented dialogue systems. In *Proceedings of the 61st Annual Meeting of the Association for Computational Linguistics (Volume 1: Long Papers)*, pages 1–21.

Shayne Longpre, Le Hou, Tu Vu, Albert Webson, Hyung Won Chung, Yi Tay, Denny Zhou, Quoc V. Le, Barret Zoph, Jason Wei, and Adam Roberts. 2023. The flan collection: Designing data and methods for effective instruction tuning.

Sean MacAvaney, Andrew Yates, Sergey Feldman, Doug Downey, Arman Cohan, and Nazli Goharian. 2021. Simplified data wrangling with $ir_datasets. InSIGIR$.

Craig Macdonald, Nicola Tonellotto, Sean MacAvaney, and Iadh Ounis. 2021. Pyterrier: Declarative experimentation in python from bm25 to dense retrieval. In *Proceedings of the 30th acm international conference on information & knowledge management*, pages 4526–4533.

Philip M McCarthy and Scott Jarvis. 2010. Mtld, vocd-d, and hd-d: A validation study of sophisticated approaches to lexical diversity assessment. *Behavior research methods*, 42(2):381–392.

Simon Mille, Kaustubh Dhole, Saad Mahamood, Laura Perez-Beltrachini, Varun Gangal, Mihir Kale, Emiel van Miltenburg, and Sebastian Gehrmann. 2021. Automatic construction of evaluation suites for natural language generation datasets. In *Thirty-fifth Conference on Neural Information Processing Systems Datasets and Benchmarks Track (Round 1)*.

Tri Nguyen, Mir Rosenberg, Xia Song, Jianfeng Gao, Saurabh Tiwary, Rangan Majumder, and Li Deng. 2016. Ms marco: A human-generated machine reading comprehension dataset.

OpenAI. 2023. Gpt-4 technical report.

Long Ouyang, Jeffrey Wu, Xu Jiang, Diogo Almeida, Carroll Wainwright, Pamela Mishkin, Chong Zhang, Sandhini Agarwal, Katarina Slama, Alex Ray, John Schulman, Jacob Hilton, Fraser Kelton, Luke Miller, Maddie Simens, Amanda Askell, Peter Welinder, Paul F Christiano, Jan Leike, and Ryan Lowe. 2022a. Training language models to follow instructions with human feedback. In *Advances in Neural Information Processing Systems*, volume 35, pages 27730–27744. Curran Associates, Inc.

Long Ouyang, Jeffrey Wu, Xu Jiang, Diogo Almeida, Carroll Wainwright, Pamela Mishkin, Chong Zhang, Sandhini Agarwal, Katarina Slama, Alex Ray, et al. 2022b. Training language models to follow instructions with human feedback. *Advances in Neural Information Processing Systems*, 35:27730–27744.

Ronak Pradeep, Sahel Sharifymoghaddam, and Jimmy Lin. 2023. Rankzephyr: Effective and robust zero-shot listwise reranking is a breeze! *arXiv preprint arXiv:2312.02724*.

Colin Raffel, Noam Shazeer, Adam Roberts, Katherine Lee, Sharan Narang, Michael Matena, Yanqi Zhou, Wei Li, and Peter J. Liu. 2019. Exploring the limits of transfer learning with a unified text-to-text transformer. *arXiv e-prints*.

Ori Ram, Yoav Levine, Itay Dalmedigos, Dor Muhlgay, Amnon Shashua, Kevin Leyton-Brown, and Yoav Shoham. 2023. In-Context Retrieval-Augmented Language Models. *Transactions of the Association for Computational Linguistics*, 11:1316–1331.

Jeff Rasley, Samyam Rajbhandari, Olatunji Ruwase, and Yuxiong He. 2020. Deepspeed: System optimizations enable training deep learning models with over 100 billion parameters. In *Proceedings of the 26th ACM SIGKDD International Conference on Knowledge Discovery & Data Mining*, pages 3505–3506.

Moritz Schaefer, Stephan Reichl, Rob ter Horst, Adele M Nicolas, Thomas Krausgruber, Francesco Piras, Peter Stepper, Christoph Bock, and Matthias Samwald. 2023. Large language models are universal biomedical simulators. *bioRxiv*, pages 2023–06.

Jost Schatzmann, Kallirroi Georgila, and Steve Young. 2005. Quantitative evaluation of user simulation techniques for spoken dialogue systems. In *6th SIGdial Workshop on DISCOURSE and DIALOGUE*.

Timo Schick, Jane Dwivedi-Yu, Roberto Dessi, Roberta Raileanu, Maria Lomeli, Eric Hambro, Luke Zettlemoyer, Nicola Cancedda, and Thomas Scialom. 2023. Toolformer: Language models can teach themselves to use tools. In *Thirty-seventh Conference on Neural Information Processing Systems*.

Ilia Shumailov, Zakhar Shumaylov, Yiren Zhao, Yarin Gal, Nicolas Papernot, and Ross Anderson. 2023. The curse of recursion: Training on generated data makes models forget.

Aarohi Srivastava, Abhinav Rastogi, Abhishek Rao, Abu Awal Md Shoeb, Abubakar Abid, Adam Fisch, Adam R. Brown, Adam Santoro, Aditya Gupta, Adrià Garriga-Alonso, Agnieszka Kluska, Aitor Lewkowycz, Akshat Agarwal, Alethea Power, Alex Ray, Alex Warstadt, Alexander W. Kocurek, Ali Safaya, Ali Tazarv, Alice Xiang, Alicia Parrish, Allen Nie, Aman Hussain, Amanda Askell, Amanda Dsouza, Ambrose Slone, Ameet Rahane, Anantharaman S. Iyer, Anders Johan Andreassen, Andrea Madotto, Andrea Santilli, Andreas Stuhlmüller, Andrew M. Dai, Andrew La, Andrew Lampinen, Andy Zou, Angela Jiang, Angelica Chen, Anh Vuong, Animesh Gupta, Anna Gottardi, Antonio Norelli, Anu Venkatesh, Arash Gholamidavoodi, Arfa Tabassum, Arul Menezes, Arun Kirubarajan, Asher Mullokandov, Ashish Sabharwal, Austin Herrick, Avia Efrat, Aykut Erdem, Ayla Karakaş, B. Ryan Roberts, Bao Sheng Loe, Barret Zoph, Bartłomiej Bojanowski, Batuhan Özyurt, Behnam Hedayatnia, Behnam Neyshabur, Benjamin Inden, Benno Stein, Berk Ekmekci, Bill Yuchen Lin, Blake Howald, Bryan Orinion, Cameron Diao, Cameron Dour, Catherine Stinson, Cedrick Argueta, Cesar Ferri, Chandan Singh, Charles Rathkopf, Chenlin Meng, Chitta Baral, Chiyu Wu, Chris Callison-Burch, Christopher Waites, Christian Voigt, Christopher D Manning, Christopher Potts, Cindy Ramirez, Clara E. Rivera, Clemencia Siro, Colin Raffel, Courtney Ashcraft, Cristina Garbacea,

Damien Sileo, Dan Garrette, Dan Hendrycks, Dan Kilman, Dan Roth, C. Daniel Freeman, Daniel Khashabi, Daniel Levy, Daniel Moseguí González, Danielle Perszyk, Danny Hernandez, Danqi Chen, Daphne Ippolito, Dar Gilboa, David Dohan, David Drakard, David Jurgens, Debajyoti Datta, Deep Ganguli, Denis Emelin, Denis Kleyko, Deniz Yuret, Derek Chen, Derek Tam, Dieuwke Hupkes, Diganta Misra, Dilyar Buzan, Dimitri Coelho Mollo, Diyi Yang, Dong-Ho Lee, Dylan Schrader, Ekaterina Shutova, Ekin Dogus Cubuk, Elad Segal, Eleanor Hagerman, Elizabeth Barnes, Elizabeth Donoway, Ellie Pavlick, Emanuele Rodolà, Emma Lam, Eric Chu, Eric Tang, Erkut Erdem, Ernie Chang, Ethan A Chi, Ethan Dyer, Ethan Jerzak, Ethan Kim, Eunice Engefu Manyasi, Evgenii Zheltonozhskii, Fanyue Xia, Fatemeh Siar, Fernando Martínez-Plumed, Francesca Happé, Francois Chollet, Frieda Rong, Gaurav Mishra, Genta Indra Winata, Gerard de Melo, Germán Kruszewski, Giambattista Parascandolo, Giorgio Mariani, Gloria Xinyue Wang, Gonzalo Jaimovitch-Lopez, Gregor Betz, Guy Gur-Ari, Hana Galijasevic, Hannah Kim, Hannah Rashkin, Hannaneh Hajishirzi, Harsh Mehta, Hayden Bogar, Henry Francis Anthony Shevlin, Hinrich Schuetze, Hiromu Yakura, Hongming Zhang, Hugh Mee Wong, Ian Ng, Isaac Noble, Jaap Jumelet, Jack Geissinger, Jackson Kernion, Jacob Hilton, Jaehoon Lee, Jaime Fernández Fisac, James B Simon, James Koppel, James Zheng, James Zou, Jan Kocon, Jana Thompson, Janelle Wingfield, Jared Kaplan, Jarema Radom, Jascha Sohl-Dickstein, Jason Phang, Jason Wei, Jason Yosinski, Jekaterina Novikova, Jelle Bosscher, Jennifer Marsh, Jeremy Kim, Jeroen Taal, Jesse Engel, Jesujoba Alabi, Jiacheng Xu, Jiaming Song, Jillian Tang, Joan Waweru, John Burden, John Miller, John U. Balis, Jonathan Batchelder, Jonathan Berant, Jörg Frohberg, Jos Rozen, Jose Hernandez-Orallo, Joseph Boudeman, Joseph Guerr, Joseph Jones, Joshua B. Tenenbaum, Joshua S. Rule, Joyce Chua, Kamil Kanclerz, Karen Livescu, Karl Krauth, Karthik Gopalakrishnan, Katerina Ignatyeva, Katja Markert, Kaustubh Dhole, Kevin Gimpel, Kevin Omondi, Kory Wallace Mathewson, Kristen Chiafullo, Ksenia Shkaruta, Kumar Shridhar, Kyle McDonell, Kyle Richardson, Laria Reynolds, Leo Gao, Li Zhang, Liam Dugan, Lianhui Qin, Lidia Contreras-Ochando, Louis-Philippe Morency, Luca Moschella, Lucas Lam, Lucy Noble, Ludwig Schmidt, Luheng He, Luis Oliveros-Colón, Luke Metz, Lütfi Kerem Senel, Maarten Bosma, Maarten Sap, Maartje Ter Hoeve, Maheen Farooqi, Manaal Faruqui, Mantas Mazeika, Marco Baturan, Marco Marelli, Marco Maru, Maria Jose Ramirez-Quintana, Marie Tolkiehn, Mario Giulianelli, Martha Lewis, Martin Potthast, Matthew L Leavitt, Matthias Hagen, Mátyás Schubert, Medina Orduna Baitemirova, Melody Arnaud, Melvin McElrath, Michael Andrew Yee, Michael Cohen, Michael Gu, Michael Ivanitskiy, Michael Starritt, Michael Strube, Michał Swędrowski, Michele Bevilacqua, Michihiro Yasunaga, Mihir Kale, Mike Cain, Mimee Xu, Mirac Suzgun, Mitch Walker, Mo Tiwari, Mohit Bansal, Moin Aminnaseri, Mor Geva, Mozhdeh Gheini, Mukund Varma T, Nanyun Peng, Nathan Andrew Chi, Nayeon Lee, Neta Gur-Ari Krakover, Nicholas Cameron, Nicholas Roberts, Nick Doiron, Nicole Martinez, Nikita Nangia, Niklas Deckers, Niklas Muennighoff, Nitish Shirish Keskar, Niveditha S. Iyer, Noah Constant, Noah Fiedel, Nuan Wen, Oliver Zhang, Omar Agha, Omar Elbaghdadi, Omer Levy, Owain Evans, Pablo Antonio Moreno Casares, Parth Doshi, Pascale Fung, Paul Pu Liang, Paul Vicol, Pegah Alipoormolabashi, Peiyuan Liao, Percy Liang, Peter W Chang, Peter Eckersley, Phu Mon Htut, Pinyu Hwang, Piotr Miłkowski, Piyush Patil, Pouya Pezeshkpour, Priti Oli, Qiaozhu Mei, Qing Lyu, Qinlang Chen, Rabin Banjade, Rachel Etta Rudolph, Raefer Gabriel, Rahel Habacker, Ramon Risco, Raphaël Millière, Rhythm Garg, Richard Barnes, Rif A. Saurous, Riku Arakawa, Robbe Raymaekers, Robert Frank, Rohan Sikand, Roman Novak, Roman Sitelew, Ronan Le Bras, Rosanne Liu, Rowan Jacobs, Rui Zhang, Russ Salakhutdinov, Ryan Andrew Chi, Seungjae Ryan Lee, Ryan Stovall, Ryan Teehan, Rylan Yang, Sahib Singh, Saif M. Mohammad, Sajant Anand, Sam Dillavou, Sam Shleifer, Sam Wiseman, Samuel Gruetter, Samuel R. Bowman, Samuel Stern Schoenholz, Sanghyun Han, Sanjeev Kwatra, Sarah A. Rous, Sarik Ghazarian, Sayan Ghosh, Sean Casey, Sebastian Bischoff, Sebastian Gehrmann, Sebastian Schuster, Sepideh Sadeghi, Shadi Hamdan, Sharon Zhou, Shashank Srivastava, Sherry Shi, Shikhar Singh, Shima Asaadi, Shixiang Shane Gu, Shubh Pachchigar, Shubham Toshniwal, Shyam Upadhyay, Shyamolima Shammie Debnath, Siamak Shakeri, Simon Thormeyer, Simone Melzi, Siva Reddy, Sneha Priscilla Makini, Soo-Hwan Lee, Spencer Torene, Sriharsha Hatwar, Stanislas Dehaene, Stefan Divic, Stefano Ermon, Stella Biderman, Stephanie Lin, Stephen Prasad, Steven Piantadosi, Stuart Shieber, Summer Misherghi, Svetlana Kiritchenko, Swaroop Mishra, Tal Linzen, Tal Schuster, Tao Li, Tao Yu, Tariq Ali, Tatsunori Hashimoto, Te-Lin Wu, Théo Desbordes, Theodore Rothschild, Thomas Phan, Tianle Wang, Tiberius Nkinyili, Timo Schick, Timofei Kornev, Titus Tunduny, Tobias Gerstenberg, Trenton Chang, Trishala Neeraj, Tushar Khot, Tyler Shultz, Uri Shaham, Vedant Misra, Vera Demberg, Victoria Nyamai, Vikas Raunak, Vinay Venkatesh Ramasesh, vinay uday prabhu, Vishakh Padmakumar, Vivek Srikumar, William Fedus, William Saunders, William Zhang, Wout Vossen, Xiang Ren, Xiaoyu Tong, Xinran Zhao, Xinyi Wu, Xudong Shen, Yadollah Yaghoobzadeh, Yair Lakretz, Yangqiu Song, Yasaman Bahri, Yejin Choi, Yichi Yang, Yiding Hao, Yifu Chen, Yonatan Belinkov, Yu Hou, Yufang Hou, Yuntao Bai, Zachary Seid, Zhuoye Zhao, Zijian Wang, Zijie J. Wang, Zirui Wang, and Ziyi Wu. 2023. Beyond the imitation game: Quantifying and extrapolating the capabilities of language models. *Transactions on Machine Learning Research.*

Rohan Taori, Ishaan Gulrajani, Tianyi Zhang, Yann Dubois, Xuechen Li, Carlos Guestrin, Percy Liang, and Tatsunori B. Hashimoto. 2023. Stanford alpaca: An instruction-following llama model. `https://github.com/tatsu-lab/stanford_alpaca`.

Gemini Team, Rohan Anil, Sebastian Borgeaud, Yonghui Wu, Jean-Baptiste Alayrac, Jiahui Yu, Radu Soricut, Johan Schalkwyk, Andrew M Dai, Anja Hauth, et al.

2023. Gemini: a family of highly capable multimodal models. *arXiv preprint arXiv:2312.11805*.

Hugo Touvron, Louis Martin, Kevin Stone, Peter Albert, Amjad Almahairi, Yasmine Babaei, Nikolay Bashlykov, Soumya Batra, Prajjwal Bhargava, Shruti Bhosale, et al. 2023. Llama 2: Open foundation and fine-tuned chat models. *arXiv preprint arXiv:2307.09288*.

Ashish Vaswani, Noam Shazeer, Niki Parmar, Jakob Uszkoreit, Llion Jones, Aidan N Gomez, Łukasz Kaiser, and Illia Polosukhin. 2017. Attention is all you need. *Advances in neural information processing systems*, 30.

Ben Wang and Aran Komatsuzaki. 2021. GPT-J-6B: A 6 Billion Parameter Autoregressive Language Model. `https://github.com/kingoflolz/mesh-transformer-jax`.

Yile Wang, Peng Li, Maosong Sun, and Yang Liu. 2023a. Self-knowledge guided retrieval augmentation for large language models. In *Findings of the Association for Computational Linguistics: EMNLP 2023*, pages 10303–10315, Singapore. Association for Computational Linguistics.

Yizhong Wang, Yeganeh Kordi, Swaroop Mishra, Alisa Liu, Noah A. Smith, Daniel Khashabi, and Hannaneh Hajishirzi. 2023b. Self-instruct: Aligning language models with self-generated instructions. In *Proceedings of the 61st Annual Meeting of the Association for Computational Linguistics (Volume 1: Long Papers)*, pages 13484–13508, Toronto, Canada. Association for Computational Linguistics.

Jason Wei, Maarten Bosma, Vincent Zhao, Kelvin Guu, Adams Wei Yu, Brian Lester, Nan Du, Andrew M Dai, and Quoc V Le. Finetuned language models are zero-shot learners. In *International Conference on Learning Representations*.

Thomas Wolf, Lysandre Debut, Victor Sanh, Julien Chaumond, Clement Delangue, Anthony Moi, Pierric Cistac, Tim Rault, Remi Louf, Morgan Funtowicz, Joe Davison, Sam Shleifer, Patrick von Platen, Clara Ma, Yacine Jernite, Julien Plu, Canwen Xu, Teven Le Scao, Sylvain Gugger, Mariama Drame, Quentin Lhoest, and Alexander Rush. 2020. Transformers: State-of-the-art natural language processing. In *Proceedings of the 2020 Conference on Empirical Methods in Natural Language Processing: System Demonstrations*, pages 38–45, Online. Association for Computational Linguistics.

Yue Zhang, Yafu Li, Leyang Cui, Deng Cai, Lemao Liu, Tingchen Fu, Xinting Huang, Enbo Zhao, Yu Zhang, Yulong Chen, Longyue Wang, Anh Tuan Luu, Wei Bi, Freda Shi, and Shuming Shi. 2023. Siren's song in the ai ocean: A survey on hallucination in large language models. *ArXiv*, abs/2309.01219.

Lianmin Zheng, Wei-Lin Chiang, Ying Sheng, Siyuan Zhuang, Zhanghao Wu, Yonghao Zhuang, Zi Lin, Zhuohan Li, Dacheng Li, Eric. P Xing, Hao Zhang, Joseph E. Gonzalez, and Ion Stoica. 2023. Judging llm-as-a-judge with mt-bench and chatbot arena.

Daniel M. Ziegler, Nisan Stiennon, Jeffrey Wu, Tom B. Brown, Alec Radford, Dario Amodei, Paul Christiano, and Geoffrey Irving. 2019. Fine-tuning language models from human preferences. *arXiv preprint arXiv:1909.08593*.

# SarcEmp: Fine-tuning DialoGPT for Sarcasm and Empathy

**Mohammed Rizwan**
Independent Researcher
Kota, Rajasthan, India
mohrizwan89.rq@gmail.com

## Abstract

Conversational models often face challenges such as a lack of emotional temperament and a limited sense of humor when interacting with users. To address these issues, we have selected relevant data and fine-tuned the model to (i) humanize the chatbot based on the user's emotional response and the context of the conversation using a dataset based on empathy and (ii) enhanced conversations while incorporating humor/sarcasm for better user engagement. We aspire to achieve more personalized and enhanced user-computer interactions with the help of varied datasets involving sarcasm together with empathy on top of already available state-of-the-art conversational systems.

## 1 Introduction

Recent advancements in large-scale pre-trained models, such as models using transformer-based architectures, have produced impressive results, as seen with DialoGPT (Yizhe Zhang, 2020). However, it is only recently that these models have had access to enough data to respond in a neutral tone and provide information based solely on the user's input. Understanding the emotional response and situation of the user is not an easy task, especially when it comes to providing an appropriate response. Early sarcasm detection methods heavily depended on static textual patterns like lexical indicators, syntactic rules, and specific emoji occurrences (Dmitry Davidov, 2010), (Maynard and Greenwood, 2014), (Bjarke Felbo, 2020). Unfortunately, these methods often under-performed and lacked generalization due to their inability to leverage contextual information effectively. Additionally, they faced issues with poor performance. Another problem is the lack of an explicit long-term memory of the conversation because these systems are trained to generate a response based only on the recent dialogue history (Oriol Vinyals, 2015) [A neural conversational model]. Recently, chatbots have faced challenges in providing inaccurate, nonsensical, or insensitive responses, largely stemming from a lack of contextual understanding and emotional awareness during conversations.

The key aim of this work is to enhance the neutral persona-based models by incorporating sarcasm and an empathetic touch. To achieve this, we fine-tuned the DialoGPT model using two datasets. These datasets include 1.3 million sarcastic comments from Reddit and 25,000 personal dialogues in which a speaker expressed a specific emotion, and a listener responded.

## 2 Related Work

Recent developments in engaging dialogue agents with a 'profile' (Saizheng Zhang, 2018) have helped the vision of contextually aware chatbots immensely. This allows models to respond by sticking with a persona, and hence, replies are more stable and coherent. Research on the emotional spectrum, including models that incorporate a sense of humor or sarcasm, is still being refined due to the challenging task of understanding the nuanced nature of sarcasm. According to the Khatri et al. (2018), sarcasm can be difficult to detect and harder to eradicate because abuse is sometimes hidden behind it. It will take much progress in the field to detect and generate sarcasm accurately. There have been models developed with the ability to detect sarcasm from user input (Devin Pelser, 2019). However, generating responses in the same fashion is not yet fully addressed. Even models with the ability to produce empathetic responses (Hannah Rashkin, 2019) do not fully capture the wide range of emotions experienced by a typical human being and respond accordingly. Another problem is the lack of an ex-



*Proceedings of the 1st Workshop on Simulating Conversational Intelligence in Chat (SCI-CHAT 2024)*, pages 66–69
March 21, 2024 

plicit long-term memory of the conversation. Typically, these systems are trained to generate a response based only on the recent dialogue history (Oriol Vinyals, 2015).

## 3 Methodology

### 3.1 DialoGPT

DialoGPT is well-suited for fine-tuning with multiple datasets due to its versatile architecture and pre-training on a diverse range of conversational data. It is based on GPT-2 (Alec Radford, 2018) architecture, making user-specific prompts more realistic. DialoGPT employs maximum mutual information (MMI) scoring function (Saizheng Zhang, 2018), integrating a pre-trained backward model. This model predicts source sentences from responses and filters out bland or uninformative text, ensuring it generates contextually relevant and meaningful responses. MMI enhances the model's ability to avoid generic replies, making its conversations more engaging and purposeful. The model also exhibits the capability to address commonsense questions to some extent, due to the rich amount of information learned from Reddit data. It also shows consistency with respect to the context in multi-turn generation, outperforming RNN counterparts and tending to be more consistent with the context. Additionally, the release of the source code and pre-trained models facilitates future research and development, providing a foundation for novel applications and methodologies. Furthermore, the model's performance in the (Yoshino et al., 2019) DSTC-7 Dialogue Generation Challenge demonstrates its potential for generating conversation responses grounded in external knowledge, making it suitable for applications requiring information-rich interactions. Its ability to surpass human responses in automatic metrics also indicates its potential for enhancing human-computer interactions in various domains. Fine-tuning DialoGPT can lead to the development of more intelligent open-domain dialogue systems tailored to specific contexts or domains.

### 3.2 Datasets

To fine-tune the Dialo-GPT model, we have used two datasets to achieve our target. We explain the datasets in the following subsections.

#### 3.2.1 SARC

The Self-Annotated Reddit Corpus (SARC), is a significant resource for sarcasm research and the development of systems for sarcasm detection (Mikhail Khodak, 2018). It addresses the challenge of detecting sarcasm in natural language processing, emphasizing the difficulty in discerning sarcasm due to its infrequent occurrence and complexity. The SARC dataset comprises 1.3 million self-annotated sarcastic statements, surpassing previous datasets in size by an order of magnitude. This large corpus provides opportunities for balanced and unbalanced label learning, enabling the evaluation and training of sarcasm detection systems.

We'll fine-tune DialoGPT for generating sarcastic text using the SARC dataset, comprising self-annotated sarcastic statements containing '/s'(sarcasm tag). This dataset includes conversation threads, responses, and sarcasm labels, serving as a benchmark for classifying statements. It comprises three essential components: the "label" indicating sarcasm or non-sarcasm, the "context" representing the parent comment preceding the response, and the "response" itself, serving as the answer to the preceding comment. By offering balanced learning tasks and methods for reducing false negatives, the SARC dataset aims to enhance machine learning methods and improve sarcastic text generation. It is freely available, fostering future research and the development of more effective sarcasm-based text generation and detection.

#### 3.2.2 Empathetic Dialogues

The dataset, Empathetic Dialogues (Hannah Rashkin, 2019), is designed to serve as a new benchmark and training resource for evaluating the ability of dialogue models to generate empathetic responses. It is specifically tailored to address the challenge of empathetic responding, which involves recognizing and acknowledging the emotional cues and experiences expressed by a conversation partner in a dialogue. The dataset is best suited for training and evaluating dialogue systems, including chatbots and conversational agents, in their capacity to appropriately respond to personal experiences and emotions expressed in a conversation. This is a perfect dataset to be worked upon because it is a one-on-one conversation between a "Speaker" and a "Listener". The Speaker initiates a conversation by describing a situation, and the Listener becomes aware of it

| Dataset | Perplexity | | F1 | | Loss | | Token Accuracy | |
|---|---|---|---|---|---|---|---|---|
| | SarcEmp | DialoGPT | SarcEmp | DialoGPT | SarcEmp | DialoGPT | SarcEmp | DialoGPT |
| Empathetic Dialogues | 101.1 | 100.7 | 0.12 | 0.76 | 4.61 | 4.61 | 0.24 | 0.26 |
| ConvAI2 | 141.6 | 144.6 | 0.08 | 0.78 | 4.95 | 4.97 | 0.18 | 0.18 |
| Daily Dialogs | 61.46 | 61.54 | 0.7588 | 0.05856 | 4.118 | 4.12 | 0.3328 | 0.2953 |

Table 1: Automatic metrics calculated on 1000 random examples from the mentioned datasets.

through the Speaker's words. Subsequently, the Speaker and Listener engage in six more additional turns (total 7 conversations). In each turn, a new emotion is given as a context, prompting the Listener to respond accordingly. These emotions consist of sentimental, afraid, proud, faithful, terrified, joyful, and angry.

### 3.3 Fine-tuning Process

Upon acquiring our datasets, the initial step involves processing the data to align with the model's comprehension. In the SARC dataset, comments labeled as "Sarcastic" are initially sorted based on their labels. Subsequently, this sorted data is formatted to feed into two distinct fields: 'context' and 'response,' ensuring compatibility with the model's understanding. Here, the parent comment takes the place of 'context,' while the corresponding response is assigned to the 'response' field.

Within the Empathetic Dialogues dataset, the information is structured around 'prompts' and 'utterances.' The 'prompt' signifies a sentence that is awaiting refinement based on the context, while 'utterance' represents the corresponding response aligned with that context. In this dataset, the 'prompt' is mapped to the 'context' field, and the associated 'utterance' is placed in the 'response' field for compatibility with the model's understanding.

The next step involves the concatenation and randomization of all 'response' and 'context' pairs using the Pandas Library. Subsequently, the entire dataset is divided into training (60%) and testing (40%) segments. To ensure model comprehension, each row's data is combined into a single string. A special 'end of string' token is inserted between individual strings, facilitating the model in recognizing the conclusion of each response within the string. This process streamlines the dataset for effective training and testing, enhancing the model's ability to understand and generate responses. Following the concatenation and randomization process, the data undergoes tokenization and is subsequently trained using checkpoints and a set number of epochs. The objective here is to fine-tune the model and evaluate its perplexity and other automatic metrics. The perplexity of a model entails evaluating the model's predictive accuracy in determining the next token within the sequence. The incorporation of checkpoints aids in the continuous monitoring and preservation of the model's progress during the training process, ensuring optimal performance.

## 4 Results

In this project, we choose perplexity as an automatic metric to evaluate the model's performance among others such as f1 score, loss, and token accuracy. Perplexity loss measures how well a model can predict the next word in a sequence of text. Lower values indicate a better understanding of the language and context. Perplexity is also reported to have a robust correlation with human perceptions of coherent and contextually specific natural conversations (Adiwardana and et al., 2020). We report the results in the table 1.

The fine-tuning of DialoGPT on the SARC and Empathetic Dialogues datasets has yielded noteworthy results. The model achieves a low training perplexity of 2.996, showcasing improved confidence in predicting the next token. We also perform a variety of experiments by training and evaluating different models. Table 1 depicts the performance of our model SarcEmp across three major datasets, including empathetic dialogues (Hannah Rashkin, 2019), ConvAI2 (Dinan et al., 2019), and Daily Dialogues (Li et al., 2017). We can observe that the fine-tuned model performs similarly to the baseline model and even better in some cases. Perplexity is reportedly reduced in two of the tested datasets, while loss on the datasets is consistently low. However, the difference is not significant when it comes to automatic metrics, but it will be interesting to observe the human evaluation results in a more realistic setting.

## 5 Conclusion

In this work, we have introduced a new fine-tuned model that incorporated sarcasm and empathy on top of a state-of-the-model. The resulting model is performing pretty consistently in terms of automatic evaluation, although it would be interesting to see it perform in human evaluation tasks. We believe human evaluation would provide us with useful insights into the domain of more engaging and empathetic human-computer interactions and potential directions for improvements.

## References


Michel Galley et.al. Yizhe Zhang, Siqi Sun. Dialogpt : Large-scale generative pre-training for conversational response generation. 2020.

et al. Dmitry Davidov, Oren Tsur. Semi-supervised recognition of sarcastic sentences in twitter and amazon. 2010.

Maynard and Greenwood. Who cares about sarcastic tweets? investigating the impact of sarcasm on sentiment analysis. 2014.

Anders Søgaard et al. Bjarke Felbo, Alan Mislove. Using millions of emoji occurrences to learn any-domain representations for detecting sentiment, emotion and sarcasm. 2020.

Quoc Le. et al. Oriol Vinyals. A neural conversational model. 2015.

Jack Urbanek et al. Saizheng Zhang, Emily Dinan. Personalizing dialogue agents: I have a dog, do you have pets too? 2018.

Chandra Khatri, Behnam Hedayatnia, and Rahul Goel et al. Detecting offensive content in open-domain conversations using two stage semi-supervision, 2018.

Hugh Murrell Devin Pelser. Deep and dense sarcasm detection. 2019.

Margaret Li et al. Hannah Rashkin, Eric Michael Smith. Towards empathetic open-domain conversation models: a new benchmark and dataset. 2019.

Tim Salimans Ilya Sutskever Alec Radford, Karthik Narasimhan. Improving language understanding by generative pre-training. 2018.

Koichiro Yoshino, Chiori Hori, Julien Perez, Luis Fernando D'Haro, Lazaros Polymenakos, Chulaka Gunasekara, Walter S. Lasecki, Jonathan K. Kummerfeld, Michel Galley, Chris Brockett, Jianfeng Gao, Bill Dolan, Xiang Gao, Huda Alamari, Tim K. Marks, Devi Parikh, and Dhruv Batra. Dialog system technology challenge 7, 2019.

Kiran Vodrahalli Mikhail Khodak, Nikunj Saunshi. A large self-annotated corpus for sarcasm. 2018.

Daniel Adiwardana and Minh-Thang Luong et al. Towards a human-like open-domain chatbot, 2020.

Emily Dinan, Varvara Logacheva, Valentin Malykh, Alexander Miller, Kurt Shuster, Jack Urbanek, Douwe Kiela, Arthur Szlam, Iulian Serban, Ryan Lowe, Shrimai Prabhumoye, Alan W Black, Alexander Rudnicky, Jason Williams, Joelle Pineau, Mikhail Burtsev, and Jason Weston. The second conversational intelligence challenge (convai2), 2019.

Yanran Li, Hui Su, Xiaoyu Shen, Wenjie Li, Ziqiang Cao, and Shuzi Niu. Dailydialog: A manually labelled multi-turn dialogue dataset, 2017.

# Emo-Gen BART for SCI-CHAT 2024 Shared Task: A Multitask Emotion-Informed Dialogue Generation Framework

**Alok Debnath**
ADAPT Centre
Trinity College Dublin
debnatha@tcd.ie

**Yvette Graham**
ADAPT Centre
Trinity College Dublin
ygraham@tcd.ie

**Owen Conlan**
ADAPT Centre
Trinity College Dublin
owen.conlan@tcd.ie

## Abstract

This paper is the model description for the *Emo-Gen BART* dialogue generation architecture, as submitted to the SCI-CHAT 2024 Shared Task. The **Emo**tion-Informed Dialogue **Gen**eration model is a multi-task BART-based model which performs dimensional and categorical emotion detection and uses that information to augment the input to the generation models. Our implementation is trained and validated against the IEMOCAP dataset, and compared against contemporary architectures in both dialogue emotion classification and dialogue generation. We show that certain loss function ablations are competitive against the state-of-the-art single-task models.

## 1 Introduction

The realm of human conversation is intricately woven with emotions, a fundamental aspect that significantly influences the dynamics of communication (Li et al., 2021). In contemporary research within Natural Language Processing (NLP) and Human-Computer Interaction (HCI), the development of emotion-aware conversational agents has emerged as a focal point. Various methodologies have been employed to handle emotions in conversation, with categorical labels and dimensional ratings being prominent avenues. These labels often find their roots in established emotion theories, such as Ekman's (Ekman and Oster, 1979) or Plutchik's (Plutchik, 1980), as evidenced in datasets like IEMOCAP (Busso et al., 2008) and DailyDialog (Li et al., 2017). Additionally, alternative corpora and models adopt unique lists of emotion words, exemplified by the EMPATHETICDIALOGUES dataset (Rashkin et al., 2019).

The "dimensional" approach to handling emotion involves the utilization of characteristics inherent in emotional speech (Buechel and Hahn, 2017). A noteworthy model in this context is the Valence-Arousal-Dominance (VAD) Model, which assesses the positive or negative sentiment, the degree of excitation, and the level of control exerted by the stimulus (Buechel and Hahn, 2016). This model has become a cornerstone in understanding and quantifying the nuanced dimensions of emotions expressed in conversational interactions. As we delve into the intricacies of emotion-aware conversational agents, the utilization of both categorical and dimensional frameworks provides a comprehensive understanding of the emotional landscape within human-machine dialogues.

In the domain of emotion-aware or empathetic conversational agents, diverse methodologies have been employed to augment systems' understanding and responsiveness to emotional cues. Some methods incorporate input augmentation techniques, thereby exposing the conversational agent to various emotional expressions to enhance learning robustness (Goel et al., 2021; Carolus et al., 2021). Simultaneously, alternative approaches integrate common-sense or pragmatic information, drawing upon broader contextual knowledge to enrich the agent's comprehension of emotions within a given conversation (Ghosal et al., 2020; Scotti et al., 2021).

Our system, **Emo-Gen BART** is a modification on BART architecture (Lewis et al., 2019). Our approach uses BART's emotion decoder attention representation to perform emotion classification as well as dimensional emotion detection. We then augment that representation to reinforce signals associated with emotion information. Our strategy implements emotion classification and regression and combines their loss with the emotion-informed generation task. When accounting for contextual information through the conversation, we find that this method makes it competitive with state-of-the-art conversational agents.



*Proceedings of the 1st Workshop on Simulating Conversational Intelligence in Chat (SCI-CHAT 2024)*, pages 70–74
March 21, 2024 ©2024 Association for Computational Linguistics

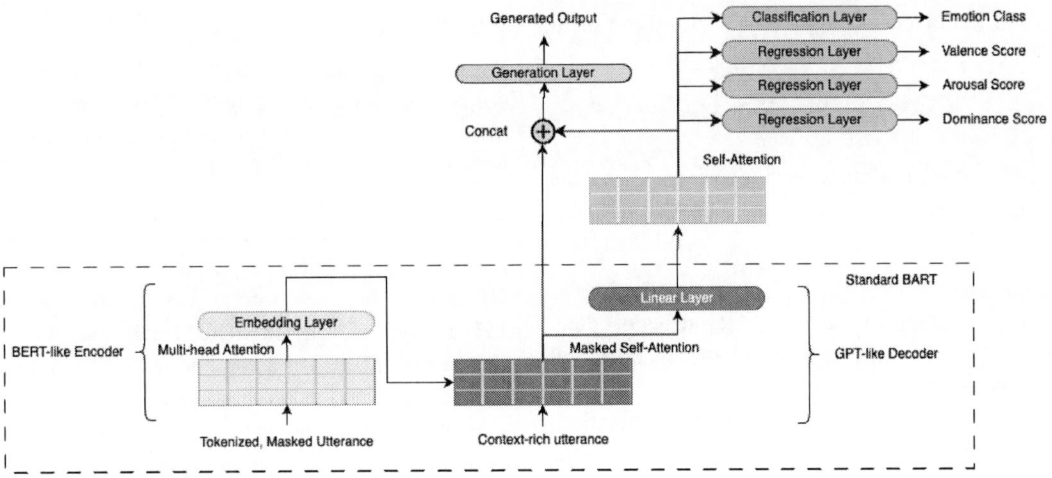


Figure 1: The Emo-Gen BART is a variation over the standard BART architecture with a bidirectional BERT-like encoder and an autoregressive decoder. Note that during fine-tuning for conditional generation, the input sentence is provided to both the encoder and the decoder. Using the decoder output, we perform multiple emotion detection tasks. The final generation layer uses the decoder attention as well as the multitask attention.

## 2 Model Architecture and Implementation

Emo-Gen BART, a customized version of the BART language model, is specifically tailored for conditional dialogue generation. The architecture of BART involves a bidirectional encoder processing tokenized and masked input sentences. During fine-tuning, this encoder utilizes the denoised input along with the encoder representation to generate subsequent sentences. For conditional generation tasks, a randomly initialized encoder precedes the bidirectional encoder during training.

During fine-tuning, Emo-Gen BART modifies the BART architecture by extracting the last hidden layer, employed to predict emotion class and Valence-Arousal-Dominance (VAD) attention scores, illustrated in Figure 1. Emotion-aware information is incorporated by concatenating the multitask and decoder attention outputs before the generation phase.

### 2.1 Loss Functions and Training Objectives

Emo-Gen BART, a modification of the BART encoder-decoder model, incorporates three key refinements during fine-tuning. Firstly, a multitask classification and regression model employs the decoder output for prediction. Secondly, attention outputs from the multitask model are concatenated with the decoder attention outputs during the generation phase. Thirdly, in fine-tuning for conditional generation, the decoder receives input as the sentence with the preceding context truncated at the input length.

Consider an utterance $\mathbf{u} = u_1, \ldots, u_M$ the model parameters $\theta$, which update based on each task.

**Classification** The objective of the classification layer is to minimize cross-entropy loss between predicted and actual emotion class values. For a batch of $N$ samples, we compute classification loss as:

$$\mathcal{L}_{\text{cls}} = -\frac{1}{N}\sum_{i=1}^{N}\sum_{j=1}^{C} y_{i,j} \log p(c_{i,j}|\mathbf{u};\theta)$$

where $C$ is the number of classes, $y_{i,j}$ is the binary indicator of where $j$ is the correct class and $p(c_{i,j})$ is the predicted probability distribution of the model for the $i^{th}$ utterance $\mathbf{u}$.

**Regression** The three regression tasks, i.e. valence, arousal, and dominance detection, are trained with the objective of minimizing the mean-squared error loss between the predicted and actual values, which is computed as:

$$\text{MSE}(\hat{y}, y_{\text{true}}) = \frac{1}{N}\sum_{i=1}^{N}(\hat{y}_i - y_{\text{true}_i})^2$$

for any predicted value $\hat{y}_i$ and any true value $y_{\text{true}_i}$ for any $i$ of $N$ samples. The predicted and actual regression value for each utterance is summed up for all utterances across a batch. So, the dimensional emotion loss can be computed as:

$$\mathcal{L}_{\text{reg}} = \sum_{d \in D} \lambda_d \cdot \text{MSE}(\hat{d}, d_{\text{true}})$$

where $D$ are the emotion dimensions, $\lambda_d$ is the weight for each regression task. For our purposes, $\forall d \in D; \lambda_d = 1$.

**Generation** The generation layer was implemented analogously to the BART decoder. The outputs of the final layer from the decoder and the multitask self-attention layers are concatenated and passed through a linear layer for generation. The input to the encoder is the current utterance tokenized, while the decoder input includes the context of the conversation.

Note that the input to the encoder and the decoder differ. For every utterance $\mathbf{u}$, there is a context $\mathbf{c} = \{c_1, \ldots, c_N\}$, which is comprised of previous utterances and responses. Therefore, the input to the generation layer may be computed as:

$$\mathbf{x} = \text{Attn}_{\text{decoder}}(\mathbf{c} \cdot \mathbf{u}) \oplus \text{Attn}_{\text{multitask}}(\mathbf{u})$$

For every input $\mathbf{x}$, the model generates a response $\mathbf{y} = \{y_1, \ldots, y_n\}$. The training objective here is also to minimize cross-entropy loss between the generated sequence and the actual dialogue response, which may be computed as:

$$\mathcal{L}_{\text{gen}} = -\frac{1}{N} \sum_{i=1}^{N} \sum_{t=1}^{T} \log P(y_t | \mathbf{x}, y_1, \ldots, y_{t-1}; \theta)$$

wherein $N$ is the number of samples per batch, $T$ is the length of the generated sequence, $y_{i,t}$ represents the predicted probability distribution over the vocabulary for the $t^{th}$ token in the $i^{th}$ sequence.

**Combined Training Objective** The training objective of the model is to minimize the total loss, computed as a weighted sum of the regression, classification, and generation losses.

$$\mathcal{L} = \alpha \cdot \mathcal{L}_{\text{cls}} + \beta \cdot \mathcal{L}_{\text{reg}} + \gamma \cdot \mathcal{L}_{\text{gen}}$$

For our purposes, $\gamma = 1$ and $0 < \alpha = \beta \leq 1$. We find that varying the relative importance of the non-generation tasks impacts generation, but causes sensitivity to initial hyperparameters.

## 3 Experiments

In this section, we describe the dataset, experimental setup, and hyperparameter information for reproducing these experiments.

### 3.1 Dataset

We fine-tune Emo-Gen BART on the IEMOCAP corpus (Busso et al., 2008). This is a benchmark corpus of recorded conversations which have been transcribed into dialogue sessions, annotated with both categorical and dimensional emotion. The IEMOCAP dataset includes video data of impromptu performances or scripted scenes of about 10 actors. There are in total 7433 utterances and 151 dialogues in the IEMOCAP dataset. At the same time, it contains audio and text transcription to meet the needs of multimodal data. In this data set, multiple commentators set the emotional labels of the utterances into nine categories: including happy, sad, neutral, angry, excited frustrated, surprised, and afraid

### 3.2 Hyperparameter Tuning

We fine-tune the model over 64 epochs with a learning rate of $10^{-5}$ and a batch size of 16. The data is preprocessed to include context of every utterance alongside the utterance to the generation layers, the input length set at 256. The multitask self-attention layers follow the dimensions of the decoder layers, i.e. 768 hidden dimensions with 4 attention heads per layer for 6 layers. For generation, we constrain the model to generate sentences with a minimum of 2 tokens, with a temperature of 1.6, a high top-$k$ vocabulary spread of 400 tokens and the top-$p$ probability sum of 0.95. Training and generation are performed on an NVIDIA-RTX2080ti.

### 3.3 Baseline Models for Comparison

We compare our results against the following baseline models:

**BC-LSTM**, introduced by Poria et al. (2017) employs a Bidirectional LSTM structure to capture contextual semantic information. However, it lacks the capability to recognize speaker relationships within the encoded content.

**DialogueGCN**, presented by Ghosal et al. (2019), organizes a conversation into a graph structure, converting the speech emotion classification task into a graph-based node classification problem. The method employs a graph convolutional neural network to effectively classify the outcomes.

Ide and Kawahara (2021), introduced a BART-based multitask framework as well. The difference between our model and their implementation is the

| Model | Avg F1 Score |
|---|---|
| BC-LSTM | 59.19 |
| DialogueGCN | 64.18 |
| Ide and Kawahara (2021) | 62.42 |
| **Emo-Gen BART** | **69.49** |

Table 1: The comparative performance results for emotion classification of our model against the baselines.

| Model | BLEU | *dist-1* | *dist-2* |
|---|---|---|---|
| Ide and Kawahara (2021) | 32.55 | 6.00 | **30.77** |
| **Emo-Gen BART** | **36.46** | **6.46** | 30.65 |

Table 2: The comparative performance results for emotion-aware generation.

use of only a categorical label for their multitask generation, and that it does not adopt the context input.

## 4 Results and Findings

### 4.1 Emotion Classification Results

By leveraging the BART pre-trained language model, our model adeptly encodes sentences to enhance the representation of utterances. Simultaneously, our multitask attention framework integrates both the inherent emotional tendencies of the utterance and contextual information. This approach proves more effective in discerning the speaker's emotion, as affirmed by experimental results. Our assumptions regarding the emotional factors within ERC find validation through these findings.

### 4.2 Dialogue Generation Results

Initially, we assess the relevance of output responses to the correct response using BLEU (Papineni et al., 2002). Subsequently, we examine lexical diversity by evaluating distinctiveness, as proposed by Li et al. (2016). This distinctiveness measure is calculated through *distinct-1* and *distinct-2*, which focus on unigrams and bigrams, respectively. We find that the *distinct-2* value for our method is lower than the state-of-the-art multitask model, which warrants further investigation.

The model has been submitted to the SCI-CHAT shared task for human evaluation and benchmarking.

## 5 Conclusion and Future Work

In this paper, we introduce Emo-Gen BART, an architecture that employs a modified BART language model to enhance the capabilities of emotion-aware conversational agents. Our approach integrates a multitask attention framework, acting as an emotion capsule, to improve the model's proficiency in identifying emotional cues during dialogue generation.

We find that this approach of accounting for several tasks including emotion classification and regression, can inform the model and improve upon baseline results. We use only a single model variation where all the loss functions are weighted equally, however model ablations which form a hyperparameter relationship between the various tasks. Finally, with multitask setups which change the nature of the architecture itself, it would be interesting to leverage LLM predictions using dataset specific signals.

## Acknowledgments

The work presented in this paper is supported the and is supported by the Science Foundation Ireland Research Centre, ADAPT at Trinity College Dublin under Grant Agreement No 13/RC/2106_P2. This work has received research ethics approval by Trinity College Dublin Research Ethics Committee (Application no. 20210603).

## References

Sven Buechel and Udo Hahn. 2016. Emotion analysis as a regression problem–dimensional models and their implications on emotion representation and metrical evaluation. In *ECAI 2016*, pages 1114–1122. IOS Press.

Sven Buechel and Udo Hahn. 2017. EmoBank: Studying the impact of annotation perspective and representation format on dimensional emotion analysis. *EACL 2017*, page 578.

Carlos Busso, Murtaza Bulut, Chi-Chun Lee, Abe Kazemzadeh, Emily Mower, Samuel Kim, Jeannette N Chang, Sungbok Lee, and Shrikanth S Narayanan. 2008. Iemocap: Interactive emotional dyadic motion capture database. *Language resources and evaluation*, 42:335–359.

Astrid Carolus, Carolin Wienrich, Anna Törke, Tobias Friedel, Christian Schwietering, and Mareike Sperzel. 2021. 'alexa, i feel for you!'observers' empathetic reactions towards a conversational agent. *Frontiers in Computer Science*, 3:682982.

Paul Ekman and Harriet Oster. 1979. Facial expressions of emotion. *Annual review of psychology*, 30(1):527–554.

Deepanway Ghosal, Navonil Majumder, Alexander Gelbukh, Rada Mihalcea, and Soujanya Poria. 2020. Cosmic: Commonsense knowledge for emotion identification in conversations. *arXiv preprint arXiv:2010.02795*.

Deepanway Ghosal, Navonil Majumder, Soujanya Poria, Niyati Chhaya, and Alexander Gelbukh. 2019. DialogueGCN: A graph convolutional neural network for emotion recognition in conversation. In *Proceedings of the 2019 Conference on Empirical Methods in Natural Language Processing and the 9th International Joint Conference on Natural Language Processing (EMNLP-IJCNLP)*, pages 154–164.

Raman Goel, Sachin Vashisht, Armaan Dhanda, and Seba Susan. 2021. An empathetic conversational agent with attentional mechanism. In *2021 International Conference on Computer Communication and Informatics (ICCCI)*, pages 1–4. IEEE.

Tatsuya Ide and Daisuke Kawahara. 2021. Multi-task learning of generation and classification for emotion-aware dialogue response generation. *NAACL-HLT 2021*, page 119.

Mike Lewis, Yinhan Liu, Naman Goyal, Marjan Ghazvininejad, Abdelrahman Mohamed, Omer Levy, Ves Stoyanov, and Luke Zettlemoyer. 2019. BART: Denoising sequence-to-sequence pre-training for natural language generation, translation, and comprehension. *arXiv preprint arXiv:1910.13461*.

Jiangnan Li, Zheng Lin, Peng Fu, and Weiping Wang. 2021. Past, present, and future: Conversational emotion recognition through structural modeling of psychological knowledge. In *Findings of the association for computational linguistics: EMNLP 2021*, pages 1204–1214.

Jiwei Li, Michel Galley, Chris Brockett, Jianfeng Gao, and William B Dolan. 2016. A diversity-promoting objective function for neural conversation models. In *Proceedings of the 2016 Conference of the North American Chapter of the Association for Computational Linguistics: Human Language Technologies*, pages 110–119.

Yanran Li, Hui Su, Xiaoyu Shen, Wenjie Li, Ziqiang Cao, and Shuzi Niu. 2017. Dailydialog: A manually labelled multi-turn dialogue dataset. In *Proceedings of the Eighth International Joint Conference on Natural Language Processing (Volume 1: Long Papers)*, pages 986–995.

Kishore Papineni, Salim Roukos, Todd Ward, and Wei-Jing Zhu. 2002. Bleu: a method for automatic evaluation of machine translation. In *Proceedings of the 40th annual meeting of the Association for Computational Linguistics*, pages 311–318.

Robert Plutchik. 1980. A general psychoevolutionary theory of emotion. In *Theories of emotion*, pages 3–33. Elsevier.

Soujanya Poria, Erik Cambria, Devamanyu Hazarika, Navonil Majumder, Amir Zadeh, and Louis-Philippe Morency. 2017. Context-dependent sentiment analysis in user-generated videos. In *Proceedings of the 55th annual meeting of the association for computational linguistics (volume 1: Long papers)*, pages 873–883.

Hannah Rashkin, Eric Michael Smith, Margaret Li, and Y-Lan Boureau. 2019. Towards empathetic open-domain conversation models: A new benchmark and dataset. In *Proceedings of the 57th Annual Meeting of the Association for Computational Linguistics*, pages 5370–5381.

Vincenzo Scotti, Roberto Tedesco, and Licia Sbattella. 2021. A modular data-driven architecture for empathetic conversational agents. In *2021 IEEE International Conference on Big Data and Smart Computing (BigComp)*, pages 365–368. IEEE.

# Advancing Open-Domain Conversational Agents: Designing an Engaging System for Natural Multi-Turn Dialogue

**Islam A. Hassan** and **Yvette Graham**
mohamedi@tcd.ie and ygraham@tcd.ie
School of Computer Science and Statistics, Trinity College Dublin

## Abstract

This system paper describes our conversational AI agent developed for the SCI-CHAT competition. The goal is to build automated dialogue agents that can have natural, coherent conversations with humans over multiple turns. Our model is based on fine-tuning the Snorkel-Mistral-PairRM-DPO language model on podcast conversation transcripts. This allows the model to leverage Snorkel-Mistral-PairRM-DPO's linguistic knowledge while adapting it for multi-turn dialogue modeling using LoRA. During evaluation, human judges will converse with the agent on specified topics and provide ratings on response quality. Our system aims to demonstrate how large pretrained language models, when properly adapted and evaluated, can effectively converse on open-ended topics spanning multiple turns.

## 1 Introduction

Developing artificial intelligence capable of natural, multi-turn conversations remains an ongoing challenge in AI research. While recent advances in deep learning and large pretrained language models have accelerated progress in conversational AI, accurately capturing the nuances of human dialogue over extended interactions is still an active area of investigation. Although competitions like SCI-CHAT provide a platform for evaluating conversational models through real-time human interactions, our focus is creating an agent for coherent, open-domain dialog across diverse topics and turns.

Our approach uses large language models fine-tuned on real-world podcast conversations, immersing them in the natural flow and back-and-forth that defines human dialogue. We leverage the promising LoRA (Low-Rank Adaptation of Large Language Models)(Yu et al., 2023) architecture to equip our agent with the ability to navigate diverse topics and engage in coherent, multi-turn exchanges.

Beyond technical prowess, we believe these agents hold immense potential to impact fields like education and customer service. Imagine a virtual tutor providing personalized learning experiences or a virtual assistant seamlessly understanding your requests and completing tasks effortlessly. However, it's crucial to acknowledge potential ethical considerations surrounding bias and manipulation in advanced dialogue systems. We're committed to developing these technologies responsibly, ensuring they contribute positively to human-computer interaction.

Participating in open-domain interactions, like those facilitated by competitions, provides invaluable real-world experience and crucial human feedback. These live evaluations, assessing factors like coherence, consistency, and topical relevance over extended dialogues, serve as a crucial testing ground for our models. Ultimately, our hope is to contribute to the overarching goal of creating dialogue agents that can converse with humans naturally, paving the way for deeper and more meaningful human-computer interactions.

## 2 Model Architecture

Our conversational agent is based on fine-tuning the Snorkel-Mistral-PairRM-DPO language model for dialogue response generation. Snorkel-Mistral-PairRM-DPO [1] is a large Transformer-based language model based on Mistral(Jiang et al., 2023) and fine-tuned on trained on the UltraFeedback dataset, providing a strong foundation for various natural language generation tasks, To efficiently adapt the large language model for our task, we used LoRA (Low Rank Adaptation Of Large Language Models)(Yu et al., 2023). MMLU (Massive Multitask Language Understanding)(Hendrycks et al., 2021) allows fine-tuning just a small number of extra weights in the model while freezing most

[1] https://huggingface.co/snorkelai/Snorkel-Mistral-PairRM-DPO



*Proceedings of the 1st Workshop on Simulating Conversational Intelligence in Chat (SCI-CHAT 2024)*, pages 75–79
March 21, 2024 

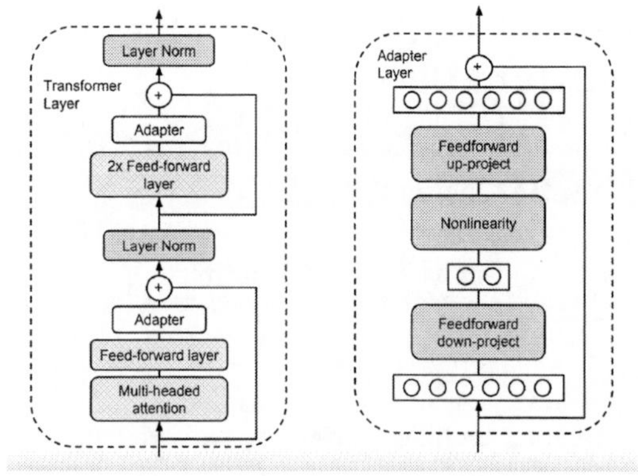


Figure 1: Architecture of the adapter module and its integration with the Transformer (Houlsby et al., 2019)

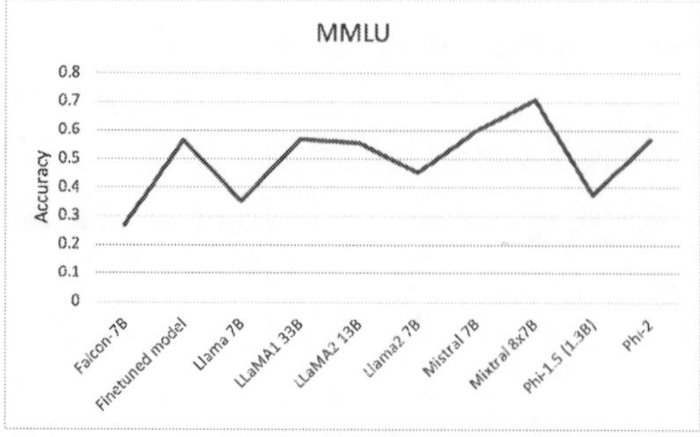


Figure 2: MMLU Performance Metric (accuracy) for the finetuned model against different Models.

of the parameters of the pretrained network. This saves on the computational cost and time required to retrain the entire massive model, it also mitigates catastrophic forgetting, a phenomenon where models tend to forget their original training due to excessive fine-tuning, by freezing the model's initial weights.

Specifically, we initialize our model with the 7B parameter version of the pretrained Snorkel-Mistral-PairRM-DPO model from HuggingFace. We then perform additional fine-tuning of this model on podcast conversation transcripts to specialize it for multi-turn conversational modeling using LoRA(Yu et al., 2023), In MMLU fine-tuning, only adapters are trained, introducing additional weights to the models while preserving the original weights and fine-tuning the newly added weights.

The architecture of the fine-tuned LoRA(Yu et al., 2023) model uses a modified transformer architecture with added adapter layers1. These adapter layers are inserted after the attention and feedforward stacks. The adapter layer itself has a bottleneck design: it takes the input, reduces it to a lower dimensionality representation, applies a non-linear activation, then restores the original dimensionality. This allows the subsequent transformer layer to effectively process the adapter output. For input, the dialogue history is merged with the latest human utterance using separator tokens. This merged history is fed into the model which then autoregressively predicts the next utterance.

During fine-tuning, the input sequences are truncated to fit within the model's context length limitation. For longer dialogue histories, we only include the most recent utterances to provide necessary context. The model is trained to generate the next utterance in the transcript given the truncated dialogue context.

During inference, we utilize the fine-tuned LoRA model and its tokenizer from the Hugging Face Transformers[2] and PEFT[3] libraries for text generation. Responses are generated based on the conversation history using nucleus sampling from the PEFT library with p=0.9 to achieve a balance of diversity and coherence in the generated text.

Fine-tuning this large pretrained model on podcast conversations allows us to leverage the rich linguistic knowledge in Snorkel-Mistral-PairRM-DPO while adapting it to generate natural, topically consistent responses in a conversational setting. The live human evaluation in SCI-CHAT will provide invaluable feedback on how to further improve the model's conversational abilities.

## 3 Training Data and Data preprocessing

Training conversational AI requires large, diverse dialogue datasets. As suggested by the competition guidelines, we primarily utilized the Freakonomics podcast transcripts dataset[4] for LoRA model training. This podcast corpus contains over 477 episodes covering economics, politics, pop culture, sports and more. The wide topical range provides natural conversational data to teach coherent, free-flowing dialogue skills. In total, the training data comprises 1 5,829 context-response pairs extracted from the podcast dialogues. On average, each dialogue contains approximately 12 turns, with 33 words per turn. The context vocabulary spans 10,194 unique terms, while the response vocabulary covers 14,550 distinct words.

[2]https://github.com/huggingface/transformers

[3]https://github.com/huggingface/peft

[4]https://huggingface.co/datasets/mogaio/Freakonomics_MTD

| Dataset Information | # |
|---|---|
| Total context-response pairs | 5,829 |
| Total dialogues | 477 |
| Average turns per dialogue | 12.22 |
| Average words per turn | 33.25 |
| Context vocabulary size | 10,194 |
| Response vocabulary size | 14,550 |
| Cumulative vocabulary size | 17,338 |

Table 1: Characteristics of the Extracted Multi-Turn Conversations Dataset from the Freakonomics Podcast.

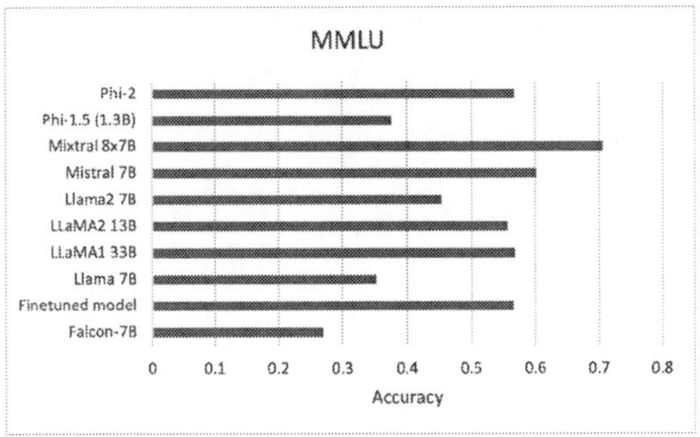


Figure 3: MMLU Performance Metric (accuracy) for the finetuned model against different Models.

The combined vocabulary size is 17,338 words, indicating rich, multifaceted linguistic interactions. These metrics characterize the structural complexity and lexical diversity of the dataset, informing the training process and performance evaluation. We scraped the raw podcast transcripts using a Python script proivded in this Git repo[5], yielding over ten thousand utterances of training data. The data was preprocessed by lowercasing, removing metadata, and filtering out very short, uninformative utterances.

In addition, the base model was pretrained on the UltraFeedback dataset, originally containing 64k prompts with 4 model completions each scored by GPT-4 for quality.

## Evaluation

In this evaluation, we used MMLU to evaluate the fine-tuned model's performance and compared it to the base model. MMLU(Hendrycks et al., 2021) is a new benchmark to evaluate AI models' knowledge and problem-solving abilities across many academic fields, without requiring additional training. It covers diverse subjects at varying difficulty levels from elementary to advanced professional. The wide range of granular topics makes it well-suited to identify knowledge gaps in AI systems. MMLU aims to challenge AI in a more human-like way through zero-shot and few-shot evaluations.

The fine-tuned model scored 0.5659 on the MMLU evaluation, while the base model scored 0.5731. Across the 57 diverse MMLU tasks covering topics like elementary math, US history, computer science, and law, the fine-tuned model's median score was 0.0202 lower than the base model on 38 tasks. However, the fine-tuned model outperformed the base model on 19 tasks. In 5 of these tasks, the fine-tuned model's performance exceeded the base model's score and the difference was over one standard deviation 4. So while on average the base model scored higher, the fine-tuning improved performance on certain specific tasks in the evaluation by a significant margin.

We also compared 2 the fine-tuned model to various other models, including (LLAMA2 7B, LLAMA2 13B, LLAMA2 33B, LLAMA2 70B, Mistral 7B(Jiang et al., 2023), Mixtral 8x7B(Jiang et al., 2024)), and conducted benchmarks using the Language Model Evaluation Harness evaluation pipeline (Gao et al., 2023) to ensure fair comparison. We evaluated performance across a diverse range of tasks in Commonsense Reasoning (zero-shot)4, including Hellaswag(Zellers et al., 2019), Winogrande(Sakaguchi et al., 2021), PIQA(Bisk et al., 2020), ARC-Easy, and ARC-Challenge(Clark et al., 2018).

This multi-domain conversational data provides a strong foundation for training our model's ability to converse naturally on open-ended topics. The human evaluation at the end will reveal how well our model generalizes to coherent, topical conversations. Additional data could be incorporated in future work to expand the model's knowledge and conversational abilities.

## Conclusion

In conclusion, we have built a conversational agent leveraging large pretrained language models and diverse, open-domain dialog data from podcast transcripts. Fine-tuning on this conversational corpus enables our model to engage in natural, wide-ranging dialogs.

At the core, we utilize Transformer architecture language models with LoRA adapters which are well-suited to modeling conversational contexts,

[5]https://github.com/hkmirza/EACL2024-SCI-CHAT-SharedTask/tree/main

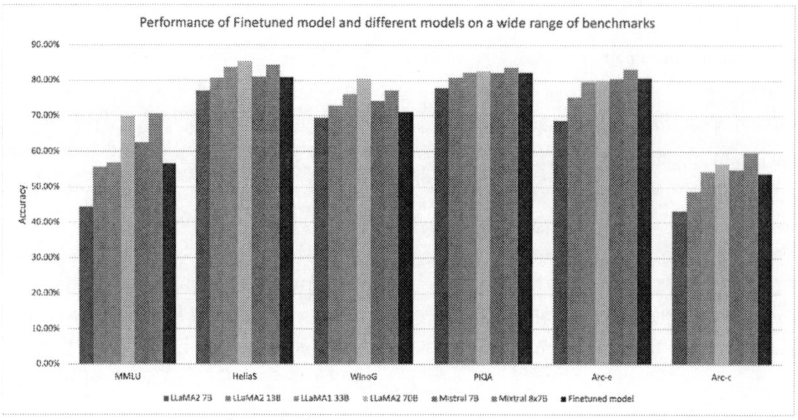


Figure 4: Performance Metrics (accuracy) for the finetuned model against different Models across different evaluation tasks.

| Model | Active Params | MMLU | HellaS | WinoG | PIQA | Arc-e | Arc-c |
|---|---|---|---|---|---|---|---|
| LLaMA2 7B* | 7 B | 44.40 | 77.10 | 69.50 | 77.90 | 68.70 | 43.20 |
| LLaMA2 13B* | 13 B | 55.60 | 80.70 | 72.90 | 80.80 | 75.20 | 48.80 |
| LLaMA1 33B* | 33 B | 56.80 | 83.70 | 76.20 | 82.20 | 79.60 | 54.40 |
| LLaMA2 70B* | 70 B | 69.90 | 85.40 | 80.40 | 82.60 | 79.90 | 56.50 |
| Mistral 7B* | 7 B | 62.50 | 81.00 | 74.20 | 82.20 | 80.50 | 54.90 |
| Mixtral 8x7B* | 7 B | 70.60 | 84.40 | 77.20 | 83.60 | 83.10 | 59.70 |
| Finetuned model 7B** | 7 B | 56.59 | 80.95 | 71.11 | 82.26 | 80.68 | 53.84 |

Table 2: Performance Metrics for Different Models (%); where *=few-shot,k=5; ** = zero-shot

| Model | MMLU |
|---|---|
| Falcon-7B | 0.2690 |
| Finetuned model 7B | 0.5659 |
| Based model 7B | 0.5731 |
| Llama 7B | 0.3520 |
| LLaMA1 33B | 0.5680 |
| LLaMA2 13B | 0.5560 |
| Llama2 7B | 0.4530 |
| Mistral 7B | 0.6010 |
| Mixtral 8x7B | 0.7060 |
| Phi-1.5 (1.3B) | 0.3760 |
| Phi-2 | 0.5670 |

Table 3: MMLU for the finetune model against different models

providing a solid foundation for language generation tasks. Further fine-tuning on the podcast data allows the model to produce coherent, context-appropriate responses during interactions. Techniques including dialog history management and nucleus sampling also boost the model's conversational abilities.

Live human evaluations will provide critical insights into the model's real-world performance, highlighting its capabilities and limitations. This human feedback will be invaluable for improving the agent's conversational strengths moving forward.

In future work, we hope to incorporate even larger models, more conversational data covering diverse topics, and techniques to improve multi-turn coherence. Conversational AI remains a very active area of research.

We believe our work is a step towards building conversational agents that can communicate naturally with humans. There is still much progress to be made, but continued research combined with establishing rigorous human-centered evaluations like SCI-CHAT will take us closer to conversational AI that is both capable and aligned with human values.

## Acknowledgements

The work presented in this paper is supported the and is supported by the Science Foundation Ireland Research Centre, ADAPT at Trinity College Dublin under Grant Agreement No 13/RC/2106_P2. This work has received research ethics approval by Trinity College Dublin Research Ethics Committee (Application no. 20210603).

| | Finetuned model | Based Model |
|---|---|---|
| MMLU | 0.5659 (± 0.1336) | 0.5731 (± 0.1323) |
| High School Geography | 0.7626 (± 0.0303) | 0.7121 (± 0.0323) |
| US Foreign Policy | 0.8300 (± 0.0378) | 0.7900 (± 0.0409) |
| Abstract Algebra | 0.3400 (± 0.0476) | 0.2900 (± 0.0456) |
| High School Biology | 0.7065 (± 0.0259) | 0.6774 (± 0.0266) |
| High School Chemistry | 0.4778 (± 0.0351) | 0.4335 (± 0.0349) |

Table 4: Comparison of MMLU for the fine-tuned model and the base model, where the fine-tuned model outperforms the base model, including standard deviation, standard error is provided in brackets.

## References


Yonatan Bisk, Rowan Zellers, Jianfeng Gao, Yejin Choi, et al. 2020. Piqa: Reasoning about physical commonsense in natural language. In *Proceedings of the AAAI conference on artificial intelligence*, volume 34, pages 7432–7439.

Peter Clark, Isaac Cowhey, Oren Etzioni, Tushar Khot, Ashish Sabharwal, Carissa Schoenick, and Oyvind Tafjord. 2018. Think you have solved question answering? try arc, the ai2 reasoning challenge.

Leo Gao, Jonathan Tow, Baber Abbasi, Stella Biderman, Sid Black, Anthony DiPofi, Charles Foster, Laurence Golding, Jeffrey Hsu, Alain Le Noac'h, Haonan Li, Kyle McDonell, Niklas Muennighoff, Chris Ociepa, Jason Phang, Laria Reynolds, Hailey Schoelkopf, Aviya Skowron, Lintang Sutawika, Eric Tang, Anish Thite, Ben Wang, Kevin Wang, and Andy Zou. 2023. A framework for few-shot language model evaluation.

Dan Hendrycks, Collin Burns, Steven Basart, Andy Zou, Mantas Mazeika, Dawn Song, and Jacob Steinhardt. 2021. Measuring massive multitask language understanding.

Neil Houlsby, Andrei Giurgiu, Stanislaw Jastrzebski, Bruna Morrone, Quentin de Laroussilhe, Andrea Gesmundo, Mona Attariyan, and Sylvain Gelly. 2019. Parameter-efficient transfer learning for nlp.

Albert Q. Jiang, Alexandre Sablayrolles, Arthur Mensch, Chris Bamford, Devendra Singh Chaplot, Diego de las Casas, Florian Bressand, Gianna Lengyel, Guillaume Lample, Lucile Saulnier, Lélio Renard Lavaud, Marie-Anne Lachaux, Pierre Stock, Teven Le Scao, Thibaut Lavril, Thomas Wang, Timothée Lacroix, and William El Sayed. 2023. Mistral 7b.

Albert Q. Jiang, Alexandre Sablayrolles, Antoine Roux, Arthur Mensch, Blanche Savary, Chris Bamford, Devendra Singh Chaplot, Diego de las Casas, Emma Bou Hanna, Florian Bressand, Gianna Lengyel, Guillaume Bour, Guillaume Lample, Lélio Renard Lavaud, Lucile Saulnier, Marie-Anne Lachaux, Pierre Stock, Sandeep Subramanian, Sophia Yang, Szymon Antoniak, Teven Le Scao, Théophile Gervet, Thibaut Lavril, Thomas Wang, Timothée Lacroix, and William El Sayed. 2024. Mixtral of experts.

Keisuke Sakaguchi, Ronan Le Bras, Chandra Bhagavatula, and Yejin Choi. 2021. Winogrande: An adversarial winograd schema challenge at scale. *Communications of the ACM*, 64(9):99–106.

Yu Yu, Chao-Han Huck Yang, Jari Kolehmainen, Prashanth G. Shivakumar, Yile Gu, Sungho Ryu Roger Ren, Qi Luo, Aditya Gourav, I-Fan Chen, Yi-Chieh Liu, Tuan Dinh, Ankur Gandhe Denis Filimonov, Shalini Ghosh, Andreas Stolcke, Ariya Rastow, and Ivan Bulyko. 2023. Low-rank adaptation of large language model rescoring for parameter-efficient speech recognition. In *2023 IEEE Automatic Speech Recognition and Understanding Workshop (ASRU)*. IEEE.

Rowan Zellers, Ari Holtzman, Yonatan Bisk, Ali Farhadi, and Yejin Choi. 2019. Hellaswag: Can a machine really finish your sentence?


# A Appendix

Table 5: Acronym Table

| Acronym | Full Form |
|---|---|
| LoRA | Low-Rank Adaptation of LLMs |
| DPO | Data-Produced-Offline |
| MMLU | Massive Multitask Language Understanding |
| PIQA | Physical Interaction: Question Answering |
| ARC-E | AI2 Reasoning Challenge - Easy |
| ARC-C | AI2 Reasoning Challenge - Challenge |
| LLM | Large Language Model |

# Author Index

**Association for Computational Linguistics**
209 N. Eighth Street
Stroudsburg, Pennsylvania 18360

ISBN 978-1-7138-9460-5

CURRAN ASSOCIATES INC.
proceedings.com